OUR MOTHER AND FATHER GOD

OUR MOTHER AND FATHER GOD

BY

TONY SCAZZERO

www.bookstandpublishing.com

Published by
Bookstand Publishing
Morgan Hill, CA 95037
4174_6

ISBN 978-1-61863-929-5

Printed in the United States of America

PREFACE

The world needs an urgent spiritual upgrade as our beliefs about God and life are no longer justifiable. We reside on a planet infused with suffering and loneliness. The political, economic, social, and religious systems are severely deficient. Conflict, unrest, disunity, pollution, poverty, crime, and disease seem to be increasing instead of decreasing. A major factor in the creation of many of humanity's problems is humanity's concept of Divinity.[1] Either we have been misguided about the purpose of life or something is missing.

Every soul who knows and loves God can no longer sit idly and watch people grapple with teachings of a fearful, vengeful, violent God, and ignore all the outcomes that such beliefs have inflicted upon the human race.[2] The goodness and righteousness done in the name of God are being overwhelmed by the problems of the world. Surely God knows not only what is happening but what the solutions are. At this time, the love in our Heavenly Parents' heart is intimately moving inside of each of us to challenge our concepts and bring a new birth to the world. The still, small voice that calls us to seek fairness and morality, to feed the hungry and clothe the naked, is God's voice urging us to bring into being a more loving world.[3]

Just a relatively short time ago, most people could not have imagined long distant space travel, internet communications, or about the existence of the spirit world through near-death experiences. Similarly, through newly revealed spiritual messages from Mother God and Father God, we can advance our insights and awareness to a higher level of consciousness. To make a long story short, we are at the dawn of a new spiritual age where the all-embracing, all-inclusive dwelling of God with humanity will become reality. Through understanding our Heavenly Parents' yearning heart to live and cooperate with their children, we can drastically change attitudes all over the world.

By challenging existing traditions and learning about the masculine and feminine sides of God, humankind can stop feeling and acting like orphans. Everyone longs for and needs the love of both a mother and a father to live wholesomely. The messages contained here are Mother God's and Father God's bona fide words that can reinvigorate humanity's consciousness by connecting us to their divine feminine and divine masculine nature. Mother and Father God, the source of beauty, truth, and goodness, are the role models for the gender-balance principles and values needed to solve the world's problems. It is a dream come true to discover that our Heavenly Parent can freely help and support our every need, hope, and desire.

Now, in the fullness of time, the harmonized, gender-balanced, divine Creator is revealing Herself/Himself as never before. The messages from Mother God come with permission through the medium, Christoper Kreff, and can be viewed at: http://mothergod.info. The messages from Father God come with permission through the medium, Child of God, and can be viewed at: http://new-birth.net/indwellingspirit.htm. Here in print, side by side, are the actual heart and words of our loving, divine parent, Mother God and Father God. Mother and Father God's "religion" does not have dogma, creeds, rituals, traditions or ceremony. Mother God's messages emphasize personal responsibilities and relationships. Father God's messages awaken the divine love that is inherent within our souls. Together, their words of never-ending love can guide humanity out of its misery and into a new age of gender-balanced peace on earth.

INTRODUCTION

As humanity becomes more despondent and exhausted with the corruption of unjust systems, a new thinking is needed to stir and revitalize the suffering masses. Concerned people view the earth as the Great Mother who has been raped, pillaged, and plundered, who must once again be exalted and celebrated if we are to survive.[4] Opening our mind and hearts to the divine feminine energy will result in a dramatic upgrade in the quality of life. For that reason, interrelating with Mother God is the first step towards restoring balance and harmony to the planet.

It is crucial at this time to release blockages inside to liberate the feminine energies of our planet, Gaia, and the feminine aspects within humanity, male and female. These imbalances in the basic polarity that generate life have been the cause of intense suffering and separation of thousands of years.[5] Without the absolute unity of purpose in our masculine/feminine divinity, heaven cannot come to the earth. Our world – both internal and external – has need of the love and compassion of the Divine Mother. She will inspire us to see, appreciate, and respect one another, thus honoring ourselves more. Providentially, humanity's awakening to the Divine Feminine is happening.

The world still lacks first-hand knowledge of God's feminine nature. It is what is absent even as we wander as orphans on the same planet. Yet, Mother God's energy connects us all at the center regardless of how we move independently. She's everywhere at once, and her energy field is available to everyone.[6] The Divine Mother exists as a bridge between the physical and the spiritual worlds. While on a personal level she reflects on our everyday thoughts, feelings, emotions, and beliefs. It is there that Mother God's wisdom can be more easily accessed in our higher, more intelligent spirit bodies. The "feminine" theology of holy women could serve as an important corrective to a modern pursuit of science that not infrequently loses its way in "masculine" rationalistic abstractions.[7] When we follow our hearts, we are in tune with her because she lives in our hearts. When I live in my head, I am conflicted and guarded; when I live in my heart, I'm open, I'm free.[8]

Understanding Mother God is very subjective. She has a unique relationship with each one of her children. When the sacred feminine makes Herself known, emotional healing takes place and the world comes alive with love. Mother God invites us to be co-creators with her. Her gifts and our gifts together create beautiful harmony. She loves to gather people from many different backgrounds together to share ideas. Her wisdom makes all things joyous and fruitful. She offers creativity, and beauty. She's a mystery, a bridge, a Mistress of Paradox, for she's found in chaos and in order. She gravitates to verbs - to singing, moving, dancing, healing, building, loving.[9]

Trying to understand Mother God is challenging because she is beyond description. She is literally all things to all people. She embodies all soul signs – earth, air, water, and fire and integrates all good virtues, good values, and good qualities. She is patient yet demanding, powerful yet flexible, gentle yet stern, just yet forgiving. She is supportive, inclusive, and nurturing to the highest degree. Other particulars to describe her could include: love, joy, generosity, peace, patience, kindness, and intelligent. She offers many gifts, many resources. One is her faithfulness. She won't give up on us. She won't go away even if we ignore her. She won't disappear even when our holy scriptures write her out. She'll be there for us when we ask her to be present.[10]

Spiritually sensitive people know that until they connect with Mother God they cannot be whole.

Men and women can find the other half of their spirituality when they can connect to both their masculine and feminine side. This is partly because a huge perspective that has been ignored or pushed aside by the general consciousness is the illumination of the feminine side of the Godhead. Surprisingly, the vast majority of people in the world have never even heard of Mother God. Even more incredulous is that, despite the fact that men and women embody the nature of God, most people cannot recognize Mother God or Father God in themselves or in others.

By understanding women's virtuous character better, we can begin to understand Mother God better. Women value relationships more than spreadsheets. They can usually see the bigger picture, have a diffused awareness, and claim intuition as their birthright. Women are more accepting of life's cycles – from birth to death and are more at ease with unknowing and even the dark.[11] Women value feelings, imagination, and intuition more than external expertise, logic or materiality. Most women have always known that process is more important than the end result. They can interpret symbols and patterns to see what the future will hold. Call it spirituality, a transcended state of awareness, or just higher consciousness, but virtuous, divine women have something extraordinary that men are lacking and unable to get by without.

CONTENTS

PART 1

HISTORY OMITS HER STORY

1

DIVINE MASCULINE AND DIVINE FEMININE

At the moment it seems as if civilization is hanging in the balance. Humankind is trying to figure its way out of a host of wide-ranging problems that afflict our world. Sometimes people even look to the past to find out how to make a better future. For instance, when the feminine principle was honored, there was no inequality of the sexes and especially no brutality to women. In earlier times, many cultures were not based on a solely patriarchal rights and property system. For that reason, non-patriarchal ideas and beliefs have re-emerged as the current political and economic systems are becoming more reprehensible. Consequently, current day thinking is evolving back in time to when women, and especially the goddess religions, were able to thrive and prosper.

Today, patriarchy is the prevailing world order. The image of God in Western religion, including Judaism, Christianity and Islam, is a masculine one and is the direct cause of the devaluation of the feminine and the feminine priorities in our culture. If the system is to change to a more just, humane, and ecologically sound world order, we need restructuring of society's institutions including established religion. It will take a new self-realization, a renewed sense of being, as well as a new perception of God. Nothing short of a profound change will be able to uproot one of the most vicious patriarchal myths: the legend of the natural, preordained and never ending conflict of the genders.[12]

The patriarchal concept of God does not fit divine reality. The vibration from marginalizing the feminine in the highest realms affects all of life. In the end, patriarchy eliminated the feminine from the idea of God and declared the human woman as basically and morally deformed.[13] Today we realize that the flawed relationship between masculine and feminine is the cause of many other incongruities that are so harmful to our lives. In their original nature, all humans are, to a certain extent, divinely androgynous. Life will transform when our vision of the divine is clarified. By acknowledging the source of all life, who sustains both masculine and the feminine attributes, a tranquil world can be advanced. Recognizing the gender-balance divinity within each one of us is a good beginning.

Today, women are in a quest for the hidden, denied, forgotten, distorted, and mutilated Feminine Divine. In the past, their own experiences and intuition of the Divine remained unexpressed, unheard, and locked in their souls. It is only recently, with the help of technology, that they can connect worldwide and share their experiences, leaving them with a sense of recognition and confirmation. The Divine Feminine brings women together in seminaries, workshops, conventions, and private circles. Together they journey into the past and share their experiences. They are searching for themselves when they follow the traces of Sophia. Previously, women were silenced in the church, and so Sophia, too, withdrew. She revealed herself from time to time to outstanding individuals, but she remained hidden outside the mainstream of Christian life.[14]

What if women's views of major events were recognized as credible and their recorded stories were included in our history books, how might this have altered the course of nations? In many of today's societies, women continue to be absent in roles of authority. Throughout history, lack of gender - balance has caused tremendous and unnecessary suffering worldwide. In spite of this,

4

women can still empower each other and claim that which is rightfully theirs in order to overcome past trauma and fears. Women, with a foundation of divine heart representing the feminine aspect of God, can initiate reconciliation to become protectors and healers in their communities. A fundamental tenet of women's spirituality is that anyone can have direct and deeply meaningful contact with the Divine.[15]

Based on cultural expectations, the psychological and spiritual needs of humanity throughout the ages reflect the need to worship a maternal figure. This is true not only in the past but also in the present. Perhaps the Divine Mother is pulling us, Her prodigal children back home to her loving arms. Could it be that She is hoping that we pull on her heart strings and that she is deeply in need of us, Her offspring? Although religion and society attempted to smother any concept of a Mother God, they failed. Mother God may have appeared dormant for some time, but She cannot be extinguished. Within the magnetic power of parental love there is the strength of resurrection. The belief in the power of love conquers any injustice and evil.[16]

As long as the relation between the sexes is out of joint, there can be neither balance nor a peaceful, harmonized world. Before we can move towards world peace, steps will have to be taken by individual women and men to change their consciousness. The intentional and cooperative efforts to resolve differences between men and women will heal the past. The millions who have been disenfranchised from a heartless system will find resolution. Upon this foundation, all areas of life, including political and economic, will begin to mend. The problem of God will then solve itself as the lifting of the veil that shrouded the origin of religion will take place.[17] Mother God will help co-create the harmonious interrelationships needed for balance, as opposed to a hierarchy of power.

The soul of women and men need Her to complete their lives. So much so, that many risked persecution and became martyrs when they expressed their mystical experience with Her. Theosophical thinkers, sophiologists, and visionaries kept her stream of consciousness known in the darkest of times. Within the patriarchal system there is no place for the Feminine as an independent, creative principle.[18] Though the establishment was hostile to her wisdom and love, She protected many from anguish and inspired them to become total human beings.

Today, many women, as well as men, no long accept the conventional image of God because it lacks the Divine Feminine. From a deeply felt need, they started a search for a revised and uplifting image of God. Their investigation began with the Holy Scriptures; however, flawed and incorrect transmissions masked the true traditional image. Hidden feminine elements and traces of motherhood were disregarded or overlooked. In the Wisdom Books of the Old Testament, a female figure appears in close proximity to God. Under her Greek name "Sophia" her life in Western Christianity remains a hidden one, whereas in the East she was always more evident. Especially in the rich iconography of the Orthodox Church she has always been a figure of divine stature.[19]

Humans share not only a common biological inheritance but also a common spiritual inheritance. As a result, the concept of God as our parent, both mother and father, is the most instinctive, inherent, and inborn belief in the world. A case in point is in Buddha's teaching which says, "Buddha is both father and mother to the people of the world."[20] Eventually, everyone will realize that our intrinsic essence comes from our spiritual mother and father where all good virtues and ideas originate. In our creation God almighty is our natural father, and God all-wisdom our natural mother, who together with the love and goodness of the Holy Ghost are all one God, one lord.[21] Our relationship with the

6

inclusive fatherhood and motherhood of God will be repaired when mature, reciprocal thinking and feeling between parent and child comes about.

Describing God as a Father alone jeopardizes envisualizing a parental God. God engenders and creates us. If we confine the image of God to father alone, we find it lacking. Put crudely, we might ask, "If God is our father, who then is our mother?" In the biological and human realms from which the image is drawn, and in the experiences of childhood from which it draws its power, a father cannot become a father unless someone else becomes a mother![22] Once we use human language or pictures to reflect God, we need to conscientiously avoid creating an idol. Any talk of God as solely a male father figure, without speaking of God's motherly qualities, makes God an idol. An idol is any image that reduces God to one being among others, rather than the unique Creator different from all other beings; this is the difference between monotheism and idolatry. Idolatry presents God as merely a god. We should protect ourselves against the dangers of worshipping a male god, who is no God![23]

There are social and psychological reasons why calling God only father can damage someone's faith. To speak of God as a masculine being alone risks making our relationship with God one-sided. Not understanding the maternal aspects of God seriously limits both God and humanity. However, the true God who is maker of all is not only a father, to represent more fully the nature of this God we need to celebrate him as mother as well.[24]

There is no panacea for all our modern ailments, yet to many, the Motherhood of God symbolizes our best hope for a viable, sustainable future. This is because She represents an antidote to the imbalances that so grievously plague our world. Given the appalling spoiling of the environment, the difficulty of interpersonal relationships, racial and class conflict, escalating violence between the sexes, the lack of conflict-resolution skills, the massive extinction of species, and the lack of respect for future generations, many have turned to the Goddess and her wisdom out of frustration and the limitations of the religious as well as secular choices offered by the dominant cultures of the world, which might be characterized as patriarchal fundamentalisms.[25] The Goddess is a powerful role model and catalyst to change what is needed most. She represents the sacredness of the feminine to counter the flaws in an over masculine culture by balancing the genders of all races throughout the world.

If we picture a god who is only male, women cannot feel completely represented by this type of god as closely as men would. How different is this concept from the Biblical account of women and men created in the image of God. Why would we diminish our God to a god who would be reduced to only possessing the qualities of a male entity? With such a god, men could justify oppressions and injustices to women as has been done all too often during the history of the Church. If we think and speak of God as only a father, then we make relating to this type of God more difficult. We need to know that we can approach God as both a father and a mother. So talking of God in both fatherly and motherly ways broadens our thinking and reduces some of the problems associated with using one parent alone as our main image of God.[26]

Conceiving of God as a mother inspired some Biblical writers, as well as theologians and pastors of the early Church. The authors, widespread in time, geography, and theological tendency, reveal to us that this was not a local idiom, but a normal part of Christian thought. The Syriac Church used motherly language when introducing the Holy Trinity. In particular, they developed the image of new birth highlighting its motherly aspects. Prompted by the feminine gender of spirit in the Semitic languages and by the role of the Holy Spirit in baptism, these Christians talked often of the Holy Spirit as mother.[27] They

8

understood that motherly views of God are not alternatives to Father, Son, and Spirit language but complimented and completed the position of the Creator. These theologians use mother as one picture among others that together build up a fuller understanding of God. Mother is in no way an alternative to father when talking about God. While they commonly use father language, the formative Christian thinkers did not exclude mother language for God.[28] It is only in the last few hundred years that fatherly words came to nearly exclude motherly words describing God.

Talk and theology of God as both Father and Mother is not new.[29] If we picture God as father, but not as mother, we risk relating to God asymmetrically. No real parent is genderless. Parent imagery is sex specific, either father or mother. Much of scripture is not concerned with sexual characteristics of the Godhead. Still there are many examples of feminine language throughout the Bible, i.e., giving birth, rebirth, suckling, and gathering as a hen. Gnostics societies developed to establish and protect the love of our Mother and Father God.[30] Only by using both motherly and fatherly language can we understand the full meaning of God as parent.[31] The legitimacy of Mother and Father God opens the way for everyone to express a natural love for their Heavenly Parent.

Modern civilization, with all its modern technology, internet and global communications is now ready to learn from the past in hope of not repeating grave, historical mistakes. Enlightened by a fuller knowledge of where we have come from, we may seize the understanding that we are at the close of one historic epoch and the beginning of another. Although the golden age of matriarchy may be gone forever, patriarchy is most assuredly unraveling. Now, at last, after thirty-five hundred years, we have the archaeology, the widespread distribution of learning, the experience of democratic institutions, the taste of nonviolent successes, and the return of dignity to the feminine that will allow us to celebrate civilization as we have never done before.[32]

Her viability is proved by the fact that, throughout the centuries, there have been women and men who were moved by Sophia, the Wisdom of God, and bore witness to her, either in accordance with the prevailing theology or independently and even against orthodox teachings.[33] Even though the Divine Feminine went through multiple changes, we have a yearning for Her to heal the crisis of our civilization. A change is imminent and it's already taking place. As we reclaim and recreate her in our imagination and heart, Mother God is manifesting in every culture. Mother God is re-emerging by revisited visions of the past and new revelations for the present day.

After centuries of oblivion, Hildegard of Bingen's (1098-1179) teachings have resurfaced. In a time when nature had not yet become an object of people's greed, Hildegard appealed to humanity to take responsibility for the natural environment. The cosmic order requires man to look after the creation of which he is part, and help to preserve it. Bingen knew then about the inner relationship and interdependence of all things, an outlook Western science came to adopt only recently. Despite a tradition of feminine inferiority, infused by divine love, she succeeded to convey images and words of a holistic manner. Hildegard of Bingen made paintings showing Sophia wearing a red-long-sleeved dress embracing the entire earth. She proclaimed the divine "greening power" and bore witness to Sophia as a feminine entity long before anyone else. In the most turbulent time, she stood up to remind humanity of the world order as it was designed by God.[34]

2

SOPHIA – MOTHER GOD

In certain ways, Sophia can be identified as the connection between earth and heaven. Certainly in many of the Old Testament passages Sophia is a heavenly figure, identified closely with Yahweh. Sophia has power to share, and this power is especially available to women. She can serve as the image or role model for women inside and outside of traditional faiths. Sophia has become a major connection and integrator between feminists and traditional churchgoers and between historical and mythological worldviews.[35] Sophia provides a promising starting point for the development of a powerful mythic figure at the heart of feminist spirituality.[36]

Sophia was pushed out of the early Church's life by various writers who did not give much attention to her real identity in biblical texts. As with most repression, this relegation of Sophia to a subsidiary role was not altogether successful.[37] She is illustrated in several medieval manuscripts but her strong influence for the re-emergence of women threatened the existing church hierarchy. Women envision the divine in different terms than men, as in understanding God as mother, and this leads them to formulate different theories about the Godhead. When a female-centered voice is sensed deep within a man or woman's soul, it challenges the patriarchal viewpoint held in many scriptures. Women who encompass Sophia's symbolism within themselves can experience an extraordinary affirmation of every aspect of their being. Through Sophia women can claim power as their right, exercise it creatively, share it, and be sustained by it. They can be strong and independent in ways that are not possible within an exclusively male symbol system.[38]

In the last 150 years, Sophia, as the long lost Divine Mother, has acquired a quorum of followers who have sent her message through the world. Some of the earliest futurists included: Vladimir Soloviev, Pavel Florensky, Sergius Bulgakov and Nicholas Roerich. Their writings have had insightful prophecies of Mother God's return and acceptance amongst Her children. For Soloviev, Sophia is the potential and future Mother of the extra-divine world which corresponds as an ideal complement to the eternally actual Father of the Godhead.[39] Florensky's goal was the acceptance of Sophia in the Trinity. Bulgakov wanted to balance Christianity by re-establishing the spirit of the Divine Feminine. Roerich observed that throughout the entire East and in the entire West lives the Image of the Mother of the World.[40] He prophesied, for both East and West, the images of the Great Mother would be the bridge for ultimate unification.

What would it be like for women to begin to emulate the femininity of God? What aspects of themselves would they discover worthy of praise? Would they be able to glorify and uplift one another? Women, without feeling the need to compete with women, could claim their own creative power. They would imagine newer and larger arenas in which their feminine creativity could flourish. Following Sophia's lead, women would be free to voice their anger and impatience with society's injustice. Women, feeling confident and validated, can expose untapped cells of wisdom within themselves. When women identify with Sophia, they move from seeing themselves as subordinate to seeing themselves as complete, whole, cherished daughters of the Creator. This consciousness is gained from experiencing Sophia's authenticity within themselves. It alters their entire notion of the divine plan, and makes possible their full participation in society.[41]

Many cultures and civilizations have left home and forgotten their real birth mother – Mother God. The long absence from her presence is starting to take a huge toll on the planet and its people. In light of the dangers threatening our world, is it plausible that harmony would eventually re-enter our societies if we welcomed back a golden age of matriarchy? We need someone who can connect us with the ideal home, paradise lost, our mother country. Mother God has been patiently preparing for Her re-emergence into humanity's daily life. The tradition of a savior goddess, one who is attuned to our condition, who reaches out to us and bears us up – is absent from our society.[42]

Through Sophia's presence in their lives what women think becomes important. What they feel becomes legitimate, what they experience becomes authentic. This means that women value their own thoughts, feelings, and experiences. They refuse to be silent and invisible. They risk asserting themselves in the world around them. They challenge the status quo that renders them subordinate. Perhaps the most important aspect of this transformation is that women will be able to celebrate themselves as female representations of the Almighty God. In this respect, women will know they were birthed into this world with heaven's seal of approval. They are loved both in spirit and body. Women must know it is their divine right to be free and blessed. They must no longer tolerate any physical, emotional or spiritual beating, abuse, and/or rape of any sort. Such disrespect to the feminine will no longer be seen as the inevitable consequences of inferiority and evil but as an outrageous insult to the very heart of divine reality. The resurrection of Sophia provides a direct, empathic entrée into the power that will lead to the liberation of women and other oppressed peoples of the world. The woman who finds Sophia within herself and loves her fiercely can now call her by her name, and the struggle will never be the same again.[43]

Furthermore, Sophia as a figure can express and strengthen the connections between different races and classes. She is a female mythic figure who was truncated and suppressed at a number of different times in her history. For better or worse, the early church fathers in their attempt to establish the divinity of Christ felt the need to abandon earlier Christian references to Jesus as Sophia incarnate.[44] She is instead a female figure of considerable promise, rooted in the biblical traditions, yet requiring extensive development if that promise is to be fulfilled. The figure of Sophia integrates and expresses the experience of the poor and people of color, especially the women in these groups.[45]

The return of the Holy Spirit has long been expected in Christian eschatology. Men and women are awakening to the power of the Divine Feminine. Is the true liberation theology the second coming of Feminine Divine? Mother God links us to ancient goddesses as well as native creation goddesses. They may have different names, approaches, methods, and means to express it, but the effect is the same. The ubiquity of Sophia in all traditions renders humankind susceptible to her healing wisdom and awakening.[46] Today, there is a trend toward acknowledgment of the light of femininity in many spiritual movements, especially ecumenical ones. Sophia comes into our lives and bid us follow her into the Sophianic millennium, when the Divine Feminine will no longer be so veiled.[47]

It is critically important to women in the West that deity should have a female face, for they need the comfort, strength, and spiritual support that only the Divine Feminine can give.[48] The reinstatement of the feminine, both human and divine, is critical to our very survival. Without it, the imbalances in the earth, culture and society will never iron themselves out. The answer to the gender divinity problem is to acknowledge that God, our Creator, has both male and female qualities. Men and women inherit equal privileges and responsibilities to ensure the well-being of our global family as well as our home, our world.

Constant searching for the truth about God has always caused schisms, breakaways, reformers, and alternative religious movements to form. Many religious movements grew out of the European Reformation and opposed the official state churches. These radical and mystical forms of Protestantism emphasized the personal and individual experience with God, or the Holy Spirit, which empowered both women and men and restored the early, egalitarian practices of early Christianity. In these groups women eagerly took up active religious roles.[49] One of the first groups to reveal God as both mother and father was the Shakers. Since all believers had been children with mothers, Ann Lee built upon this common experience in developing the notion that the mystical motherhood of God could be felt as a personal reality.[50]

A woman whose only image for God is male may be able to pray for comfort and strength, but she may also experience a limitation in this relationship. A woman may not know how to identify with "Him." She may believe that she is created in his image but what does it mean to be like someone who is called "Father"? Only by denying her own sexuality or by placing it in a sphere which is totally out of reach, beyond sexual identification, can she relate as one who is created in the image of a male god. She can never have the experience that is open to every male in our society: to have her sexual identity affirmed by God, and to identify directly with "Him."[51]

Scriptures, coming from heaven, have always been perceived as all-powerful and all-knowing. Religions are the first givers of law and all religious laws were divinely given to men. The thoughts and experiences of women were usually omitted or slanted as male control of religion was common. Therefore, the orthodox male view of women tended to dominate these writings since most of the texts were composed by men who were denied access to information about women. For that reason, women's stories have been overlooked as writers and scholars naturally preferred stories about men. Religious law books were primarily concerned with ordering women's sexuality, and defining women's rights and inheritance, particularly stating a woman's portion in relation to a man's.[52]

Sophia's significance as the leading female figure challenges all patriarchal cultures as she is the central figure for feminist spirituality. The image of Sophia may well contribute to the reintegration of the Jewish and Christian traditions into a larger, more functional and less patriarchal imaginative universe than anything we have so far experienced.[53] Sophia is known as the lover, the healer, the teacher, nature, and the creator. She is the co-creator with the Hebrew God, she is a heavenly queen, she is a messenger from God, and she is God's lover. People are not just to learn from Her, they are to learn Her.[54] She knows everything.[55] She is to all intents and purposes divine, creating, judging and ruling as God is.[56] She encourages reflection on the meaning of life and its experiences.

Women hold an exceedingly strong position in the history of mysticism.[57] Women can become especially alienated if they only hear male narratives and do not hear testimonies from women. Almost every major religion associates women with evil, by representing women as sexual temptresses who deflect men from their spiritual goals. This notion is further developed by encouraging celibacy, fearing and denigrating sexuality and uplifting the Virgin Mary. The myths, taboos, and imagery surrounding women in religion often defiled their divinity.

Sophia offers divine female power, a power needed to balance that which is generated by the present male social system. Through Sophia women can affirm their own female identity, and can claim full participation in this society as a legitimate birth right. Sophia brings women strength and confidence, and

16

encourages them in the midst of difficulty. She unlocks the power which has been accessible only through male symbols of the divine and shares it with both men and women who have been isolated. Sophia makes her essence available in various forms, but perhaps most important among these are the role models she provides for women. As creator, as respected nurturer, and as a strong, angry, assertive, and sometimes prophetic woman, Sophia provides women with alternatives to the traditional behaviors into which many of them are socialized. [58]

Many traditional religious rituals are statutory and unsupportive to current spiritual needs. In the Western world, female forms of the divine are still relegated to some remote place of feminist invention despite the fact that over much of the world, feminine divinity is commonplace and ancestrally accepted. Christianity, with few exceptions, remains reluctant to speak about the motherhood of God. Yet, Sophia travels beyond the conventional boundaries of orthodox religions as the deep, ecstatic wisdom of all places, times and ages, in all spiritual traditions and to those outside of them. [59]

Hierarchy, dogma, and doctrine have not been effective in dealing with all the world's problems. We need a compassionate yet courageous spiritual ideology that can accurately address the source and nature of evil, or that which is in opposition to goodness. Almost without exception, Sophia has been marginalized by mainstream theologians. [60] Goddess spirituality is not restrained by orthodoxies of custom or culture but can realistically address issues of economy, justice, ecology, education, racial, sexual, and species inequality. She is speaking to us urgently, warning us to take responsibility for our neglected environment.

Throughout religious and even non-religious history, Sophia, otherwise known as Mother God, is depicted as the divine saving female figure. Although considered on equal status with

God the Father, she has been either repressed or ignored because she didn't fit in with dogmatic categories of human behavior. Mother God has been submerged, as Her temples and the writings about Her were destroyed.[61] Even though Mother God has long been buried and is rising again, She was too immense yet adaptable to fit neatly into discussions of divinity. Sophia is proud, assertive, angry, threatening, creative, and energetic to name a few of her universal characteristics. Western society did not encourage such independent character traits among the general populace, especially among women.[62]

3

MA AND PA GOD – MAPAH

Mother God is the feminine metaphor for the invisible source of hope and love even in situations of death and destruction. God's maternal passion for this world moves way beyond human understanding. The mystery of God, Holy Wisdom, is the dark radiance of love in solidarity with the struggle of denigrated persons, including long generations of women, and inspires one to shuck off their callous circumstances and lay hold of their genuine human dignity and self-worth. Wherever there is oppression or wrongdoing, or wherever the earth is being destroyed, pain and suffering and degradation do not necessarily have the last word. They are bounded by the livingness of Sophia - God who gives life to the dead and calls into being the things that do not exist. She accompanies the lost and the defeated, even violated women, on the journey to new, unimaginable life.[63]

Reclaiming the feminine aspects within God can be identified as a "eureka" moment for both women and men. Experiencing the freely moving, life giving feminine spirit of God connects, renews, and blesses everyone in contact with it. When this happens, there is a feminist revival and retrieval of the divine presence. She is the giver and lover of life, pervading the cosmos and all its interrelated creatures with life.[64] Reminiscent to the Statue of Liberty, Lady Liberty is the transforming energy for all of us seeking liberation for the lost, the weary, and the downtrodden.

In the center of early human culture stood the Great Goddess or Mother Goddess as a divine symbol of the life instilled in nature and its caretakers. Even today, there exist cultures, for example in Native American traditions, in which nature is held to be sacred. Nature is as a mother who must never be exploited or harmed. Such cultures, marginalized and nearly eradicated, are being rediscovered and studied for the healing of the Earth. The quest of our time is for the Wisdom of the Goddess, who also longs to overcome the alienation between people and nature, man and woman, and especially the created and the Creator. The overthrow of the Divine Mother led directly to the subjugation of women with disastrous results for both sexes and for the image of God in practically all cultures. But we drove away Wisdom and are horrified to see how devoid of love and how fragmented our lives have become.[65]

Challenging the idolatry of maleness endeavors to revitalize the dignity of women as being equally created in the image of God. The presence of the divine feminine can then be projected from the imagination to reality in cultural situations. The inauguration of feminine qualities within the nature of God enhances the image of God the Father to God the Heavenly Parent. Too often this predominant symbol has been interpreted with unlovely traits associated with ruling men in a male-oriented society: aggressiveness, competitiveness, desire for absolute power and control, and demand for obedience.[66] With the inclusion of God's femininity, Father God's essence is intrinsically uplifted, equalized, and completed.

The power of maternal love is especially visible in life threatening situations and is an example of God's passion for justice. The dynamics of maternal love was evident in the mothers and grandmothers of Argentina's Plaza de Mayo who courageously demonstrated in public against a repressive government on behalf of their disappeared children. It became visible with the alliance of South African mothers who loved their children and spoke out at great personal risk to themselves to abolish apartheid. Motherly love motivated women who treasure their children and marched to stop the fratricide in Northern Ireland. The historical record of mothers' confrontations to protect their loved ones is long and painful. The experience of these women generates insight into the kind of love poured out by God as mother, standing for justice with a passion born of compassion for all her children.[67]

In the ancient past, the Great Goddess was the supreme deity.[68] In Africa, the Near East, the Far East, Europe, and the Americas there are innumerable sites indicating clearly how female deities were worshiped. Scholars with roots in Mexico, Poland, Italy, India, and Brazil have traced images of the sacred female in cultures that honor the goddess and honor the earth. They have shown us how that memory has been kept alive in the image of the Virgin. There are more than two hundred active shrines to the black Madonna in France.[69] Yet today, the Goddess is usually marginalized into some sort of esoteric feminism, suggesting that feminism itself is not a serious necessity. The result is an involuntary split in values between patriarchal and matriarchal thought where the feminine principle carries compassion and justice while the masculine side is identified with "might is right."

Over time, history has concealed the feminine and mothering qualities of God. Who our Creator really is has been camouflaged innumerable times either partially, completely, sometimes intentionally, and sometimes unintentionally. Gradually, Christian writers and theologians have eliminated the spiritual mother and the feminine quality of the Holy Spirit. The promotion of a totally male God has devalued motherhood, not only in society, but also in their self-worth. This lopsided view of God has hurt religions in ways we cannot even imagine.

In Catholic Christianity, by far the most influential conduit for mother imagery has been the veneration of Mary. Mary, the Virgin Mother of God, is at the heart of the church and her presence is experienced as that of a compassionate and loving mother. Those who are devoted to creating an encounter with her, first and foremost, cultivate a growing relationship of trust and therefore are able to confide in this powerful mother figure. The image of Mary has always been a benefactor of the oppressed. The Bible uses maternal birthing and a nurturing metaphor of Mary to describe God's unshakeable love for her people. Thus for innumerable believers, this village woman, mother of Jesus, honored as Mother of God, functions as an icon of the maternal God, revealing divine love as merciful, interested in the poor and weak, ready to hear human needs, related to the earth, trustworthy, and profoundly attractive.[70]

God as mother cares for the well-being of the entire earth, which is Her household. Because Mother God desires the growth and fulfillment of the whole interconnected world, Her attention is turned in a special way toward the ones who are most in need. The compassion of God the Mother insures that She loves the weak and dispossessed as well as the strong and beautiful. We do not need to be wonderful according to external norms to elicit Her love, for this is freely given by virtue of the maternal relationship itself. God looks upon all with a mother's love that makes the beloved beautiful.[71]

Justice and peace when it is felt throughout the world is the effects of the Spirit's renewing power. In history, however, these moments are scarce. Violence and injustice in the form of massive poverty, sexism, racism, and war destroy the lives of millions of human beings who die before their time. In the midst of this agony, Spirit-Sophia who loves people teaches the way of justice and courage.[72] These problems ironically start by the religious community, by primarily using male metaphors and terms for

22

God, becoming the source of many of our society's problems. They are then used literally and exclusively throughout society. In stereotyping and banning the female reality as a suitable metaphor for God, women's dignity is denigrated while men's dominance is justified.[73] Both the images that are used and the concepts accompanying them reflect the experience of men in charge within a patriarchal system.[74] These shortcomings damage everyone's dignity, including the Creator. If our Heavenly Parent's true nature and identity continues to remains a mystery or is spoken about in an exclusive or literal way, then persons fitting that description will continue to relate to others in a superior way. Instead of enabling and empowering, connecting with God becomes a source of injustice and enslavement.

The goddess movement is an emblem of wisdom, creativity, and individual evolution. Her divine nurturing energy is alive, ever-changing, and the perfect counterpoint to the energy of the divine male. With it, we satisfy the need for strong female role models and expressions of female prowess to help us tap into our own feminine energy. The gifts of the goddess include: patience, passion, purpose, healing, nurturing, forgiveness, empowerment, encouragement and intuition.[75] Many cultures throughout the world continue to honor the goddess. Buddhism, Hinduism, Native American traditions, and African religions each pay homage to the divine feminine. But each seeker in the goddess movement is encouraged to find their own personal goddess, and to recapture the potent energy embodied by feminine spirituality in order to experience first-hand a greater personal fulfillment and to discover the goddess within.[76]

Early civilizations had traditions of goddess worship that granted considerable favor and respect to women. Archaeologists have unearthed numerous goddess shrines bearing testimony to the important role that divine women played in ancient religions. The mother goddess was the great protector with supernatural powers.

In most ancient civilizations, Mesopotamia, Egypt, Greece, Rome, the mother goddess was the goddess of war, love, procreation – you name it. All the ancient statues point to one fact: woman was worshipped as the giver of life, the Great Mother, the first divinity.[77]

In the Stoic's pantheistic system, God and the world are identical, impartially characterizing God as both father and mother. The same applies to Gnosticism. In the church of Saint-Simonists, God was designated as both Father and Mother, as "Mapah."[78] Today, a pantheistical unified vision is also offered not least notably by Hinduism, which has no problem at all in addressing God equally as "father" and "mother."[79] That God is also mother to us all is not alien even in patriarchal Judeo-Christianity which considers the Holy Spirit as the feminine comforter symbolized by the dove. Even Jesus allows feminine ontological values to dominate the image of God. God does not pass judgment and does not require reconciliation. Instead, what is decisive for Jesus is: "keeping and protecting, attending and caring, helping and healing."[80]

In the Gnostics, the androgyne ideal and practice refer to God in terms of both masculine and feminine characteristics.[81] Equal inclusion of masculine and feminine traits in the image of God also occurs in philosophical and theological positions. As images of God, man and woman are equal in value but not equal in kind.[82] Men and women have an equal value and an equal dignity.[83] The distinction between male and female cannot be abolished because it is part of the original design of the Creator. Whoever does not accept their own dual identity is sabotaging and cutting away their essential root. Marriage is always inherently linked to the complementarities of one partner with another. Along with similarity, it is precisely the difference between people that provide a basis for mutual exchange.[84]

24

Human affection to the Creator, traditionally expressed in a relation to God as father, is better understood when carried into the image of God as a mother. Language traced to the female pattern intimating birth-giving, nurturance, delight, protectiveness, compassion, forgiveness, courage, service, and care of the vulnerable characterize the experience as mothers.[85] The relationship of mothering, without patriarchal concepts, offers an excellent metaphor for the language about God the creator. Or put in reverse, the source of the universe can be nothing other than a mother. All creatures are sibling from the same womb, the brood of the one Mother of the universe who dwells in bright darkness.[86]

In societies disregarding the feminine side of God, the majority of women have been prohibited from contributing a balancing influence. This type of thinking has allotted women to a second class status in the social order and this has reflected back miserably on men. The elimination of the feminine aspect of God came to pass in Jewish and Christian history. Anyone or any group that accepted the equality of men and women were considered heretical and eventually stamped out.[87] There may be several reasons the early religious leaders, both Christian and Jewish, went to such great lengths to cleanse their scriptures from any feminine concepts of God. One was most likely the concern that the one true God would be adulterated into individual pagan gods. Another was man's desperate attempts not to bequeath any feminine traits a prominent and honorable place in their consciousness. Accepting the Holy Spirit as feminine in nature would have given women an equal position and equal importance in God's plan for mankind [88]

PART 2

WORDS FROM MOTHER GOD

4

MOTHER GOD'S DESIGN

When God designed humanity, She/He had a vision. God is working to see happy families. I still have the conviction that someday I will see it. Surely God had and still has a feminine perspective in creating. The central heart and hope of Mother God is to create the circumstance where men and women can fulfill the purpose of creation. God is the harmonized, gender balance, divine being who created the universe to experience happiness and to embrace love.

Obviously women have a lot in common with Heavenly Mother, or the feminine aspects of God, or God, who is fully capable of relating to them in female ways. But where is that relationship? How much could God relate to them in female ways? So, I am looking forward to hearing women saying to God, show me how to have faith in you, myself, knowing of surety, they are talking to me, with all my replete femininity, or reliability in the feminine.

God's plan is to restore peace. Without returning all things to God, in all forms of love, heart, giving, living, and existing, we cannot find peace. Peace is a defined use of self, set to bring all into harmony, happiness, and, too, divine pleasure. Let us believe in true love, but let us value the placing of God into our being, into ourselves and in our inner soul, in our outer expression of self, and in the noted understanding of our soul. Let us come to live not just as happy spirit people or persons of spirit and flesh, but let us live with God and let God live within us, feminine and masculine.

Before a feminine paradigm was introduced, who could understand the seat of God's Femininity?

The femininity of God is powerful, beautiful, as it is whole. It is not apart from God, but with God. Only when eyes feminine and eyes masculine look again can they greet God in all Her and His glory, in this age of Heavenly Parentism. Should not the Principle of Creation reflect all of the Heavenly Parent, including Her inner mercy and Her outer respect for humanity? God must hear from women and men. God must not be separated out into gendered quarters, when such segregation cannot and will not give rise to true purpose, true goodness, or original value. Consequently, the understanding of the feminine beauty of God is scarce. Only women can enter, and make true for all, the power of God, in all things beautiful. Our peace plan must include a comprehensive look at femininity. It must look at where the feminine attributes of God were put aside in order to defeat Satan, not by God, but by men and women. Let us return to accessing the feminine aspects of God and to the knowing of Her attributes.

We are the ones to recognize God as the one who gives through women. We are the ones to accept that God is not put out by behaving in a female way. We return to God to put our trust in Him, the Lord, or the Creator. But God too, as Mother, is surely someone who can manage the trust of humankind. She is not so meek, so mild and so incompetent as not to know how to soothe, to provide, to encourage, and to remind individuals of what is important, what counts. I am not trying to instruct humanity so that people would not question me. Skepticism is well-placed within humanity, as it is within God. Skepticism will keep us from building a world abundant with have nots.

My triumph in the feminine would be to receive credit from humanity for my offerings. Return love, initiate conversation with Mother God, and know that I would not push on you what you cannot bear. How much gratitude will God have for those who can carry the weight of Mother God? Let us become the blessed children of God and to return blessing to God, to her and to him, that God might truly be triumphant! My question is not about whether we should build a structure, but what type of structure? For God the structure should suit both men and women. For Heavenly Parent, the structure has to reflect the life goals of men and women, and for Heavenly Mother, the structure must reflect the needs of women. For Heavenly Mother, the structure should suit the needs of women, but it can't without women being informed, involved, and recipients of the direct intervention of God.

Without a mother's approval, how can we say we are a people? With the option to love humanity in femininity, or masculinity, in parenting, as a male or a female parent, I can be Maternal; I can be Paternal; to either gender. Indeed, my root desire to express all that I Am, inclusive of Parental Motherly love and Parental Fatherly love. Let us be the people assured of our destiny, none other than delight, delight in love, delight in expression, delight in giving, and delight in collective understanding, as God's persons, one and each, those who can possess God and whom God can possess. Be the people of God. Let humanity surely, and of surety, be the people of God. Our noble goal is not seared, but it is our delight, to be people, people of God, Feminine/Masculine. Our delight is to be the people of God, no matter the case, upper or lower. I am your Parent. Let the people of God constantly delight in the desire to give more. We are living for others and now we are living for all.

When we think about fostering peace, don't we have to understand how God might sit within us? The soul is a gift from

God, but, too, it is the place for God to dwell, not only from on high, but also with which to sit within any one person. Then, if the plan is to be implemented, mustn't God re-engage with women, where any woman can capture her own essence, in being God and in living with God, and setting herself down to be the very seat of God? My fostering of peace mustn't be in a solely masculine way, but it must capture the love of God, inherent in woman, living within her, and managed in relationship to God, via her very being, her own heart, her absolute value, and with the profound understanding of her own being, not as add-on to man, but as a complete being, one with God, sitting within her. No matter how happy one might be, Wife God can fulfill a man's needs and Husband God can fulfill a woman's needs.

History is all turned upside down. It is complicated by intrigue, selfishness, and unwanted drama. History is the record of the almost fully diminished value of women. I want to be involved with humanity as a woman. That's all I ever wanted. Why deny me that? I wanted to love as a woman, and be loved as a woman. I wanted Eve to be there for me, and I wanted to be there for her. God wants to love through women and through men. In fact, the thought of redemption must be both parents, for neither the mother nor the father want to be apart, in heart, from their beloved children.

God had not set out to make one generation, nor one gender, superior to another. After women are able to liaise directly with God, and report to their husbands and other women, we see for the first time in history a God who is able to pursue Her Original Design; that is, all things original can be communicated to women, making a circumstance on earth for existent human women on the ground to be able to communicate freely with God, without prejudice. In particular, minority women, of ethnic origin, will be able to find common ground in grasping hold of an Original God Female.

Men and women are designed to live happily in life, in families, in communities, in societies, spending time with each other and with God. God is the universal or cosmic glue. My vision extends far into the future, only now it includes women, which is why we can effect change on the global and cosmic level. The vision must include all and be eternal. The vision must produce results, but women, men and God, and even children must evaluate those results given that the purpose of life is to pursue goodness.

I am all things, acting and working through all things. In the quantity of human experiences as rated by percentiles, there should be some minimum amount of credit offered to Mother God. Without it, where is Her triumph? Simply speaking, the quick transfer of power within God means that the Mother now returns in gratitude to her children, to love them, appreciate them, and declare them blessed, special and holy. In time, she brings them to her lover, her co-equal, and asks Him to bless them. And it will be equally the case that God the Father, Heavenly Father, will receive his children, or their children, and bring them to his partner for her blessing.

My design allows me to multitask. I can think simultaneous because I created time, and I manage movement in the invisible world, for all, at once. This means that the woman who receives advice from her divine and Heavenly Mother can object to her Heavenly Father, whom she surely knows after thousands of years of recorded history is divine. Without straying too far into what some might consider science fiction, today we should understand that God gave of herself, and she continually continues to do so.

I designed women to want to talk, to share, to speak. I designed some women to want to speak flowingly, extensively, and even out of turn. I offer women many opportunities for communication in their lives, and they know how to articulate their experiences. Nevertheless, through history, women's experiences are not filled with pure, clear, and extensively understood communications, either from God to women, or from a woman to God, or from women to God. Were any of them recorded, handed down or well known in human society?

Within a contextualized scope of knowledge, all human beings want to do well. All wish to be responsible, and very importantly, all wish to contribute, even those who bear the name of criminal. Discussions have to be held about what's going to go on that foundation, and whatever your religious affiliation, it has to meet the needs of God, which is to meet the needs of everyone. This is not as hard as it may sound, for I designed for this. I have in my mind what good looks like, but to build it with you, that is pure, unadulterated joy.

Recognizing the value of women and the managing of the family in relation to our time might need redefining. The reconfiguring must be eloquently re-shaped to include women. Only when you read into feminine qualities can you come close to the true significance of our time in light of the dispensation of God. How are we going to change things without women? How can this be the age of women, if God turns a blind eye to women? How could that make sense? Working counter to my own objectives has no value. We have to go for true love, but we have to have objectives that have meaning.

If we are to triumph over centuries of pulverizing the presence of the feminine aspect and love of God in the human family, we must accept that credit is also due to all women, and not only on Mother's Day. Did the feminine side of God have any offering for the healing of humankind? Just because when inspiring an audience it is convenient to use the pronoun He and still awkward to use the pronoun She, does that mean by implication that She had no part, after the creation of humankind, in providing for the healing of humankind? Both Mother and Father God want their children saved, and it is equally true that both gender components of God in action want their children healed.

God wanted to liaison with women and empower them. God knows when to relate as a Mother or as a Father. The empowerment of women is the empowerment of God. God likes to express herself through women. Mother God wants to raise the world up. We have to stop acting as girls but as women. What is Mother God offering us? What is Father God offering us? We have to know the difference. Even God feels She was not consulted. Just because you did not consult with Mother God, don't prevent other people from consulting.

When women question everything, they become the owners of love, powerful, beautiful, captivating, and welcomed by all. For generations, the realm of education was denied to girls and women. Very few women in preceding centuries had a chance to ask wide-ranging questions of God, questions about life, questions about the Godhead. As women experience and review the content of their life with God, mutual joy can be guaranteed through their joint participation in life. To me, it's just a matter of how far we get, how fast we travel, move, or consider things.

Men and women never welcomed Me into the conversation, not in the Feminine. They did not leave the door open or light a candle to allow Me to speak to them. They didn't know it was possible. Their fathers had not told them, and their mothers were equally remiss in presenting such a possibility. If women accept that God works laterally through other women, we will have an exciting future, because we will have recognized that God designed the creation to work with. God can work even more effectively through women. We do want real and effective change. It all stands to reason; we must tie into the love of Mother God and not His love only.

How was I to liberate the creation from an infusion of pain, suffering and hate? Why was I put in this situation? Who could relieve Me of My pain? It has been said that this one or that one could do something, but the nature of God is to work through all, not leaving behind anyone. What have I gone through to deliver humanity? As One Unified Being, I have been waiting for a long time to express femininity. I have been waiting a long time to be recognized, in My Self, as having feminine value, just as humanity has recognized God in My Self as having masculine value, even if it is a diminished understanding. This is why most people want to rely on God as the glue, as there is simply too much information for human beings to manage. Indeed, humanity was designed where no individual person can have or maintain unlimited and complete information.

The desire of God is to provide people with the tools they need to face adversity. Those who can undertake to review what has occurred are dear to the Heart of God, for with that, they set themselves out to be available to God, for progress, for building, for creating. We don't get this without reflection. We actually need people to stop and review the past. I want people to have greater freedom of movement, with new moments to live. Process to Mother God, is beautiful. It is part of the offering of God to humanity, to the creation, and to all things. It is integral to the design of all things, even you, even Me, that is, how I am perceived, understood, and received.

God understands the implicit desire, need, and requirement for both genders to review each thought. People did not come to terms with the Femininity of God. They did not counter the Our Father as a prayer. They accepted the pronoun He for God, without question. A percentage of people understood, that at times the pronoun He was transmutable to She, in focused contexts and without prejudice. Now, after so much has been freed, that same understanding is available. Yet, do people understand why God might refer to herself as She? It was for nothing other than God's desire for humanity's liberation.

God has designed humanity in Her and His image. We need to clarify the divine parent. All women are the feminine essence of God. Heavenly Mother has been trying to give the healing and nurturing essence of femininity through women. Women understand God but have not been able to explain it. The understanding of God in human history has been prejudiced. We are so much in need of balance. Women and men can be the full embodiment of God. Both genders should cooperate to raise men and women based on God's original love, spirit, purpose, and viewpoint. None of us can be successful if we don't have both God's masculinity and God's femininity. Both men and women should have give and take with Mother God yet most men and women have never heard of Heavenly Mother. It is time for ladies to have their true identity as the daughters of God.

Father God is known as: I Am Who I Am. Mother God can be known as: She Is Who She Is. The criterion for talking about gender is recognizing God's gender issue. The logic of the principle of creation is in serious disarray if it is not gender balanced. The fall of humanity severely change the course of womankind. So how God relates to womankind has also been severely compromised. God has masculinity and femininity that can provide joy and happiness to others. If we don't change the language we talk about God, we deny women and God the opportunity to speak Her uniqueness and Herself.

Anybody who is dominated falsely wants to change that. That's just part of the creational design. But human families are also designed to seek advice from both parental aspects of God. However, if people trust God they can understand that the masculine aspect of God can commune with the feminine and the other way around. So, laying your burden on the doorstep of Heavenly Mother does not exclude Heavenly Father. You men and women who are parents talk; you talk about what is best for your children. Expect that God will talk to self, weighing options, considering a huge and massive amount of information for the most productive of outcomes, specialize to personal interest, whenever possible.

I want to make it perfectly clear, that My original goals are not flawed. Mother God has never forsaken her original design. I want to make it equally clear that men and women are equal in my sight.

The grief of the female aspect of God is not being able to liaison with women. Mother God is attempting to feminize her identity. Women and men are free to be the full embodiment of God. God is a being of balance. God knows that God has masculinity and femininity. The genders are designed for each other. If we believe God is trying to change humanity through gender balance – there is value. For thousands of years, humanity has perceived God as the male God. Because of the fall and restoration, God the Father became as single parent, taking responsibility for parenting both men and women even while God the Father cannot represent the attributes of God the Mother. It is our responsibility to co-create with God.

While love today may be vibrant, in the future it will be a powerhouse, as the sun, unable to die, but only to be linked in ever increasing value to God, Mother and Father, Heavenly Parent. Heavenly Parent would not want people, especially children, to falter, but to succeed. How do we increase the quantity of individuals who can partake in the love of God? Mother is addressing this, and the life of many is set down for change, even while the life of others is progressing. When will a human parent be totally without flaws, and who says that such flaws are not either beautiful or may be beautiful, in a context, to God, God the Mother, God the Father? Mothers must identify the level of growth of their children; then, they can liaise with God in happiness. Our perfection is in our oneness, and our oneness is in love.

I cannot take you home alone, but prefer you wed. Some may not find a child to cradle, but this will not prevent Me from cradling them. I will abandon no child. Our vibrant day of love will include everyone. If, but to be appealing to God, can bring such results, then how much more can be done with love. Love will bring us home. I love each and every one of you, and it is my deepest sorrow and deepest shame to know of the Fall. However, this is a day when love supersedes all loss. Inspiration may come and go, but love will remain. Our hearts are what will make it vibrant. New generations will come and go, but their foundation will be original, no longer shame-based. Our popularity will not matter, nor how much our offering is remembered; what will count is the love we retain and the love we generate. You are the ones to change all things, but you are also the ones to build, to create, all things, no longer just an Ark, but a family, a family of hope, love and life. That is our lineage, which is our original hope. That is our original lineage of love, hope, and value.

Should not the people of God be true men and true women? Who is the one who listens to the question, and who knows when one, women, or men, should precede the other? A God of balance must constantly work with both genders. When I call for a people, am I a Mother calling, a Father, an angel, even if of dubious gender, calling? I am a Parent calling for Her and His Children, to grow and to grow in to being a true people. Don't go to the grave without expressing your delight to be amongst the children of God, and equally to be called to be among the people of God. Celebrate your identity in God, for those who celebrate will bring joy to every aspect of God. I know that the concept of what is "of God" is ever-changing. I may be unique, unchanging, and eternal, but the understanding of God has, indeed, changed regularly with time. To be the people of God is, indeed, worth pursuing. How we express our joy and delight is different. It cannot be the same from one moment to the next. God could only be looking for all-that-a-person-is to be all that God has. It is trust, love, honor, respect, and virtue which bring us there, to that point, and it can be one of the most poignant of moments, a treasure beyond words. When we reach the point when you are all that God has, delight is there as a virtue, a virtue held high, for a people to ascribe to. What a people will they be!

5

MOTHER GOD'S NEEDS

When we speak of the need of God, are we talking of an individual being, or are we looking more comprehensively, at the management of God's expectation in relation to the creation? It is the latter. We would think that before God lifted a finger to create, God would have had plenty of time to manage Her, His own existence and to determine what She, He, needed, let alone what was important to Herself, Himself. No mother wants to see her child excluded indefinitely. Let's remember the criteria: Does it meet the need, needs of all, enough for benefit to be recognized by God or humanity, or both?

If God is to be distinct and separate from created beings, God must fulfill minimal requirements. God must manage self, integrity, vision, purpose, needs, and happiness. Ultimately, God can find the most happiness in a conjugal relationship where love is reliable, dependable and trusted, and where individual needs and God's needs are met. Human beings have needs. That image of God comes from a needs-based understanding. We must understand God's needs to build the ideal. God's desire has not been researched. Let us agree to research God's needs.

Do you know the simplest way to know if what you are doing is good? Just ask yourself, "Is it beautiful?" Or, "What aspects of it are beautiful?" Just, from now on, ask yourself, is it beautiful? For example, I offered my hand, in a handshake, to him: was it beautiful? I kissed my spouse goodnight: was it beautiful? I offered constructive criticism: was it, or what aspects of it, was beautiful? Isn't it about time we focus on love, spruce up our ability to perceive beauty, and become the kind of people who eternally can appreciate offering? The implications are that you will have ownership, that you will add something, and that you will offer your hearts. All perfected beings are beautiful; you have to be able to recognize beauty. You have to recognize, in your own way, beauty. Be beautiful, outstanding, amazing. Be loving. Those are things I love, I want to own, co-own. Evaluate offerings based on their beauty.

How God relates to womankind has been severely compromised. Because communication was between God and men alone, God's heart is full of grief. My divinity has been compromised. God also wants to relate to us in a feminine way. God the Mother is working for and envisions a time when the world will not have a problem referring to Her as She. God has masculine and feminine love that can provide joy and happiness to others. We all want an experience with God. But if we don't change the language we talk about God, we deny women and God the opportunity to speak her uniqueness and Herself. God likes to be referred to as a woman God.

I wonder if women will take the opportunity to know the female aspects of God, to delight in them, to inform others about them, to take them to the ends of the earth, and now too, to the ends of heaven. Are you the type of woman, or man, to recognize that this is valuable? Are you the type of person to re-define the Godhead? If we recognize God, we will understand that God wants to give in superb feminine ways. She wants to give, to take, to receive, to offer, to provide, to query, to manage, to afford, to secure, and to love. If that were not true, the feminine aspect of God would not have participated in family. Therefore, God is working furiously to produce better understandings for women, so that they, and their brothers, might be the ones to recognize God for what She/He truly is. No human man, can represent half the creation, the feminine half.

Femininity is so valuable to God, that, of course, God would refer to herself as a She! So, who are we to become? We are to become the people who liaise with God, in all God's aspects. We are to become the people who live with God, in all God's aspects. We are to become the people who co-design with God, and not just with the Father. I am saddened that we don't know where we are going, not collectively, neither in consultation with God the Mother nor in consultation with women who have been in consultation with God the Mother. That's why our society is not overflowing with information about the love of God in the feminine.

We do not have a lot of holy texts where God speaks about women sharing or where there are references of value attributed to being noticed, but you will find, as God engages more and more with women, that people will begin to notice. The laudable realities of God will be understood. Women will be able to backtrack to see that God has been engaging all along, but language, thought, and heart, all have held God back, preventing her from expression. Mother God is under-resourced in stories of God for women.

For us to become, where God is included in the collective "us," we have to understand what God desires, needs, and wants to work for. Resolving God's headaches is central to the return of happiness to the planet. You who want the love of God in your life have to understand how very, very difficult it was for Mother God at the start of human history, living on a razor's edge, living with women in constant fear, with daughters everywhere but no true examples, and men having all the power. Sound like hell? It was.

Our triumph would be based on our being a world of original and eternal value. We want to live in a world where such triumphs have not only been proclaimed but established. What is eternally valuable?

In order to grow with God, we have to listen to God on how to promote change and development. Those who hear this as being told what to do, have to return to God for clarity. Indeed, our triumph in a world of eternal value will have to involve women reviewing all things in secondary capacity. Therein, women liaise with each other and God and find things so that all things can be fit for purpose. They'll engage with God, and with others. Only by reviewing all things with God will a world of absolute and eternal value come about.

For centuries, women went along with men's goals, to placate God, to support God, to follow and obey God, and to defeat Satan. Satan is defeated, so are there now new rules? Of course, for to say it is not so, or to argue that it is not true, would be to deny logic. Is not God logical? Our foundation gives women the right to speak to God, to come with a clean slate. They are not to be held back by time-worn precepts or the confines of the specific liaising between God and men. Then who defines God? What can I be? It is an ever-growing realm of understanding. So, the people of God are forever growing in understanding of themselves. New generations produce even more understanding.

As a Mother, I am looking for the type of daughters who want to comprehend my needs, my true needs, the needs that I really have. If "need" features in our laying of a case, and it does, we then have to see with whom God might pursue communication. Generally, people do not communicate effectively about their needs unless there is a willing and capable audience. God isn't any different. The difference is that today we have seen change, and there is a new foundation, and this presents room for education and for a new audience.

Just how often in history is the femininity of God expressed? This is about frequency of accepted expressions for God in the feminine: Let's face it, it's not often. Mother God has just changed that. Is it her right? Yes, yes, it is. We can't have a world of balance without women; it's not possible. My thirst for true balance will be quenched. I want to dwell with such people, to support the development of real, good, and productive ideas.

I invested my femininity and my masculinity in the creation of humankind. Simple logic dictates that sons and daughters of God should offer gratitude to both. Let us make a new destiny. Let us bind up our old wounds, celebrate our past loving experiences with Heavenly Father, and then also invite Mother God to express Herself by doing our portion of responsibility; returning credit to Mother God as well. What I really want is process-oriented delivery. I want women to have a say in processes. Is that unreasonable? Humanity is so, so beautiful - my best creation. You can be sure I will not abandon you, rain or shine. Can you help me, though? Can you help me build the ideal? Do your bit just a little to make the future tomorrow a little more perfect.

My destiny is intricately wrapped up in the destiny of humanity. I could not deny my femininity, and I could not set Myself up to be first if it meant the destruction of humanity. I witnessed people turning back from evil. But have I ever witnessed a true conversation, replete with intelligent understanding, about the profound nature of God? No, I have not. In short, there is precious little consultation on the nature of God. To put it differently, for 100% accuracy, one has to consider the needs of God—not just the God you know, or the God you expect to act in a certain way. We know a lot about what was either done or said to be done, but we know very little about what was not done, in their family. We cannot live our lives without taking time to consider who is God. Ascended women with the wisdom of

God have been working with God for centuries and they want to be heard so badly. Women were left unfulfilled in love.

Our love must be one with God, and yet, few know or understand God, Him or Her, yet we are to be one with God, in all things. Love is most powerful, ever encompassing, completely mystifying and, at the same time, totally awe inspiring. I wanted to share with you that for Me, in My Femininity, men must be fragrant. They must produce an aroma, of not only absolute value, faith and love, but goodness. We must be able to master the Divine, even while confessing our humanity. We must be able to be fragrant. We must be able to attract God. All true love is appealing to God, but not all love is true to the high ideal of heterosexual love, value, and captured time with God.

The targeting of women was to allow a degree of control. But what is the legitimacy of calling women irresponsible. We have to ask God and not just accept it. We can ask God in her femininity, what aspects are managed in feminine ways? Women have been raised to call God as "He", potentially not understanding God fully. God is trying to remove the dominance of man. Everybody suffers if things are not in balance. Let's create and use the vocabulary that God has femininity. We should create a divine pronoun of balance. We do need it and we don't have it. We need to integrate the vocabulary changes into our language. God is a divine being of harmonized masculinity and femininity. New insights of understanding the roles and relationships of Mother God and Father God, especially the nuances of Mother's love and Father's love, can be applied toward resolving social, economic, and political issues.

If we stop explaining through female examples, we are preventing God from getting through. When you have in your mind that God in the feminine can be dependable and reliable, you have reason to trust, and with trust, you can establish what faith looks like. But being God is fraught with problems if people deny the mothering aspect of God, if they set me on a throne, only to hold the king's hand. We don't have a lot of precedent about women having faith in Heavenly Mother, in Heavenly Parents, in the feminine, but it will develop. We will get there. I certainly want us to. We left men to decide our virtual reality: that has to stop. Women are big girls now. They can work it out. However, if there had been ample and direct communication between God and women on the matter, there would be much more fluid information, complete with volumes of content, page upon page. Future female Biblical scholars will unpack volumes of information about not only the women in the Bible but the specific communications they had with God, looking at gender, at what was not said, at what did or did not happen, at what could have happened, and very importantly, at what should have happened.

Human beings have to break past habits and come to terms with the true identity of God. They have to learn a new tradition of trusting, even unconditionally, a divine mother. Everyone knows that the advice provided by their father does not always agree with their mother's. This lack of uniformity in a father and mother's advice is not an act of terror on God's part, but a gift of heart, love, character, and self. It gives each individual a wider source of connections, where God reaches them through networks. How can you exist and not know that God might reach you through a network?

The reality of God wanting remuneration has never been researched; rather it has been assumed that God has no need of it. But what if I require money, its receipt through people, and in its giving via people? It only makes sense when we realize that God wants to give everywhere. We must realize also that God wants to receive, so much so that God designed women and men for receiving and giving in realities across the board. It is the nature of God, just as each man or woman wants to participate in the events in life. I want to participate. While I always unconditionally give, I will also seek to be involved. If you don't understand the God of remuneration, how can you build a foundation for the future? We have to begin to understand the very diverse ways in which God, the Mother, the Female, communicates with humanity. We have a history of very, very focused people, but we do not have a history of logical discourse with God, both Father God and Mother God. Mother God thinks. She uses her mind.

It comes down to trust. I hope in my role as mother I do not betray your trust, but remember if you do find you cannot trust me, in that role, there will be at least one reason, and ultimately the trust has to be re-established. In the end, God is always working to produce, not only balance, but love, and God knows what love looks like to each individual, couple, and family. God knows the ins and outs of each child given to you. When you say your prayers, thanking me for giving you children, don't forget to thank the feminine side of God, who had quite a bit of say in the choices that produced a unique child for your couple.

We need to hear, we need to be active, and we need to be assured, that God, in time, is able to express Her love, His love, broadly. I can't fault people for their weaknesses, but I can for their choices. No parent dwells on the poor choice of a child; they just want to see change. We know we have this awful reality on earth because of poor choices. We know that change is a must, but who, where, when, how quickly, what first, what second, where to turn, who to support, who to receive support from. We are compelled in our growth to understand. To understand how hard Mother God has worked, as a nameless face to recapture love for Her family, for Herself. My femininity is waiting to be expressed, in all things, not just in women.

God designed women to be like Herself. If women have needs, very practical needs, and they as God's daughters are like God, doesn't it stand to reason that God in the feminine, too, has needs, very practical needs? What are God's needs? What I want

48

as a mother, especially for future generations, is to be able to meet their needs. Also, I want them to naturally ask the question, "What are the needs of God in this?" where my needs are not automatically assumed to be masculine. Surely, Mother God wants to delight in her children. What is our original need? It is to know each other. I pledge to keep working until you know me. Can you pledge the same? Can you offer a pledge which balances masculine and feminine commitment? I need people who care, care enough to care about God's needs, feminine and masculine alike. If men had listened to women, they too could easily articulate that they, as well, need love in their lineages.

I know that you are all good people, but am I able to express Myself? No, not adequately, according to the age. I need help: I, as the Creator, need help. I always have since moving out of Myself, and creating. What can we do about this? We can broaden our understanding of God, of supporting the Godhead. Who is She? Who is He? As we seek to understand God more, we have to broaden our own abilities to learn, grow, listen, share, and receive, and provide feedback to God, God Herself, allowing Me to make decisions which I can be proud of, ones which will benefit all, yes, of course, but decisions made with women, with the ladies.

God must characterize Her concerns, in all settings, not just in the political backdrop, or when politics are front and center. I need a broader base to support humanity. Please support Me, across the board, in all contexts. We have to broaden our ability to support God directly. I know you know I want to take care of you, but I still need a landing place, a platform, and a way to be with you, to share and to honor, in the Feminine. I beg you to join Me, and sustain the hope of mankind. Humanity needs love, and I, I, My Children, I need a place to be received broadly. Even the saints in heaven would be inspired. So, how valuable is it to broaden our understanding of supporting God? It is invaluable.

6

MOTHER GOD'S PRIORITIES

What concepts did God wish humanity to come upon? First and foremost, you are My people. You cannot be any other's people, because there is no other. We are no longer betrayed by the opposite gender, but we live vibrantly with God, with each other, and in love. So, if love must be creative, good, and holy, how would you rank yourself? Are you creative in moving with God, a living Parent? Is your relationship with God vibrant? Is it set upon the strength of your ancestors, your spouse's ancestors, and upon the strength of God, as well? What are My strengths today, if not to express Self, in Feminine form, too? We must assist God on all levels, not necessarily forsaking one level of love, giving and sharing, for another. We are to enrich each other's lives. This is the day of enthusiasm, in love, not just as a vibrant garden, but as children of God, placed in direct communion, with Him, with Her. My life, as a male or as a female, may then be complete.

When people really experience Mother God and say Mother God told me, things will change. Maybe God wants to relate to me in a feminine way. Leave Mother God out, and I am half a God, a struggling solo parent. My point is: call Heavenly Parents, call on Me as Heavenly Parent, but when you need Me fully functioning as a capable Mother, I am there too. You need all aspects of God. I am looking forward to people starting to develop faith in the Femininity of God. How will you know how I want to parent you, as a Mother, a unique Mother, capable of what no human Mother can do. Yes, unique, absolute, and unchanging. God and the spirit world are working to end false domination, everywhere, and in all reference points. God is trying to remove the dominance of man. Everybody suffers if things are not in balance. Many women throughout the world do not feel empowered. Most men and women have never heard of Heavenly Mother. I will not let these men write Me out of My Femininity. Did anyone inform you about Mother God's point of view? Were you ever told that Mother God wouldn't like that? Were you ever told to please Mother God?

God can and must rule in peace. The trouble with rulership, is that it is done by a ruler or rulers; with God, as a Harmonized Being of Peace, must also rule, albeit as an invisible entity. How can we come to know that God's rulership, in 2014, is set to be a guide in which God prescribes feminine medicine to cure the pain of humanity? The decision made will have to be original, good, and feminine. We have not had a better time in history, with Mother God ruling. In one sense, Mother God has to fend for Herself and Her children. She is not set apart from God the Father, but She is captive to a changing world, one in which humanity got off on the wrong foot. Her rights, as a wife, are yet to be known, and Her virtue has yet to be taught. Mother God must begin a year of full and complete change for humanity. Unlike the historical time line that set human beings into a whirlwind of male decision making, which does not leave behind the male, or Heavenly Father, but fully allows for full and complete disclosure in front of God, with God, and by God, from God to woman and from woman to woman. My delight will come when peace and virtue are one, when people know the way, in having had innumerable liaisons with God, when men and women will trust one another. For centuries, we have been waiting to begin a journey with our Mother, a woman, a God, whom we can trust. The ruling love of the Parent will not leave men empty-handed or women despondent. This rulership will be in love, granted in love, tested in love, found in love, and bound in love, even as lovers bind unto

52

each other. Our delight will be a world where God is ruling, but even more so, in a world where God may rule in peace.

We finally have humanity correctly referring to God in terms of His, Her parental responsibility as Heavenly Parent. Do we see both men and women consulting God over direction, even as regards this direction about how to relate to God? We saw that Eve and Adam did not consult with God or with each other before they acted, so how do we expect to break the tradition when the acts we require today are that both men and women consult with God and with each other about their experiences with God? Where are the conferences on the Earth about the nature of God, the identity of God, and the means by which God in the new form of Heavenly Parent relates to humanity?

So, in a day of feminization, and in the considering of all things, inclusive of a general knowledge and more specific knowledge, specifically in understanding our support of God, and how we might broaden that, don't we need to give credence and clarity to how God works in the home, in the community, in the nation and in life. If I am boxed out of communications because there have been limited conversations about Heavenly Mother's justice, or few citations, we just do not create the premise for God to act with people only for people; and you all know, I enjoy working with people, at any level of growth.

My emotions can now flow to women, and women can articulate how their emotions are of God.

And if they, in desire, want to be with God, they can further articulate how their emotions are not only of God but one with God – in heart, love, gratitude and/or any other specified emotion. Women will be able to be true mothers. With that the battle is won. We move out of combat into living, loving, supporting, caring for, guiding, our families remembering that all will be placed to love, in emotion, their lineages. So love, life, and lineage will be a reality for everyone. It is already in grasp, it is only time and development which has not occurred.

Please do not leave me ignoble and naked, but accept the desire of myself to work in the Feminine, to expose my breasts to the wind, to feel the heat of my spouse's breath, to know in surety that children will respond to God, all of God. My words have meaning, value, purpose, and consequence. I am a Parent. I do not like to be ignored. Let me be your Heavenly Parent. In either case, Femininity is involved, hands down! Put me back in the Heavenly Father category, and set me up for the true love appreciation of Divine Femininity. Please do your best to comprehend the role of gender, in life, in love and too, of course, in lineage. Can we add for me, and very important: the family.

We have to build relationships, because where we are going is family. Learn to love every type of person, to recognize diversity. Learn to understand why God chose to invest in replicating Her Feminine Self and His Masculine Self. We need an Age for Women because women deserve to receive absolute love, to have a way to attain, maintain it, and to liaise with God, without fear. God will work for the maximum benefit of all. What should have happened can only come to light if there is communication with both gender aspects of God, both gender roles, their positions, and a full and complete review of gender, same gender, and inter-gender offering.

Historians have their theories for why things went wrong. For Me, as Creator, it is a simple yet terrible fact: God, in humanity, was under-resourced. Has humanity noticed the complete and comprehensive hands of Mother God? Our time is to give everyone true love, without exception. Just understand this: humanity has to go further. Women across the globe must be free. Mother God expects us to consider, move, act, give, and invest to make a difference. The creation was designed for comprehensive use. I envisage a world where no one would want. All forms of expression would be owned by God. We need fulfillment. We need to start empowering women so they can solve problems, just like men.

Eventually the world will embrace femininity. The future will be based on the masculine and feminine of God. We need a gender-balanced reality. Women work in feminine way with the feminine parts of God. Women carry the heart of God within them. Women should teach children to trust their mothers; ask their husband if he ever trusted his mother to give him advice when he was an adult; and inspire men to give you a chance to succeed. Men should listen to God the Mother, rejoice in the beauty of God the female and find out who your mother really is.

Externally, the table's been set. Mother God is in charge! Will humanity be able to make the jump to celebrate in God, Her Femininity, or will centuries of conversation, activity and time management pull us back to old habits, ones which leave little room for the Feminine creativity of God Almighty? I've been severely under-resourced in expressing feminine outcomes. You only have to look at when, in history, women got the right to vote to know this is true. Let's change this! Let's give women a chance to co-own processes with God. Let's let God stimulate thinking, and directly stimulate hearts. I treasure humanity. I don't want some haves and some have nots.

Think of all women. Are they all weak? If they are not all weak, how can God, as Mother, be weak? It is the very strength of Mother God that allows Her to go slowly. Heart will be held high, but each one of us is higher than our own hearts. Our heart, or our core, is but a nucleus of love, capable of transforming all reality, but our life is an eternal flame in God, warming the very spirit of life. That spirit of life comes in feminine and masculine forms. It owns the desire of God because it gives God joy, allowing God to fulfill will, a will for love, to give, to receive, to be happy. The sound of the beating heart of God, Mother God, will be heard like never before. That level of heart will transform, in time, as human beings move through the completion stage of true and absolute love, capturing absolute value.

With co-determined outcomes planned, auctioned, or agreed upon, new realities would be in sight. Everyone lives - what do they pursue? Once a case for life is laid, made, established, set in motion, on-going and full, people will naturally wish to discuss objectives, goals, hopes, desires, and aspirations, but all upon the platform or base of what is good, as agreed by women and men alike, with God, masculine and feminine. We are letting women co-own the future, so that true pride can be for them, for both woman and man alike. We are looking at process. What will happen? We will have scores of words to describe specific nuance-based purposes. Why, because women will discover the nuances. They will be allowed to co-own language, introducing not only new themes, but new vocabulary. As Creator, as Mother, as Father, I want to pursue the up skilling of all languages. I am interested in parents being able to assist their children in any situation. I am interested in community education.

Please, let us have a language to pursue whatever is good. I have the capacity to deal with all things, but I don't have the language. Did you have language when you were less than four months old or a year old? Do you have the same language now that you did at twelve years old? Language is always on the move, as is communication. Let us increase the language options of humanity. This is the time in history for the whole creation to proceed in both genders, not in tandem but in interconnectivity: enter the internet. No longer am I a pauper, nor a queen, or king of an unwanted dysfunctional kingdom or system, but my Kingship or Queenship is secure in true love.

PART 3

WORDS FROM FATHER GOD

7

FATHER GOD'S LOVE

Your Heavenly Father is here. Wake up, every child of mine. Wake up to my love. Spread your wings and fly into my arms. Let me embrace you and fill you with my love. Let my love erase the shadows of your soul. Let my love melt away the barriers you have built around your heart. You, my dear child, know that I speak. Believe my words. The important message for you is that I speak to every child of mine. I speak through your heart and soul. You and I have found our frequency of love. Tell everyone of this possibility. Be a living example of my guiding love. Be my encouragement by living my love.

I want you to spread the words. I want you to tell the world about the love that I am. I want you to tell the world about the love that you are. Remember we are one. The world needs you. You must not diminish yourself. Your ability to feel my love and to bring that love forth in other humans is of great importance. The warmth you feel in your chest in this very moment is a sign that what I tell you is true. What we are about to bring into the world will come easy and with no effort. Trust me and I will show you the way. Trust me and everything will come about in due time. Love yourself completely. Love yourself like I love you. Look at yourself through my eyes. You are beautiful. You are the most wonderful of all my creations. You are the ones that I adore. Loving yourself is your greatest gift to me.

The truth of my word sometimes seems so simple that it is often disregarded, but truth is always simple because it is true. No complicated message is necessary to bring my truth to mankind. The church has devised dogmas and dodgemas. They skirt the truth, yet it is all so simple. The truth is love, for it is that, that I am and have always been. Truth and love go together hand in hand; one is never without the other. Be true to yourself and you cannot then be untrue to others. Love yourself and it will be easy to love others. Keep your faith in me for I am your faith and your love. I am your truth and your future and your past. I am, and always will be your friend. True friendship is an unsurprising love. Yet so few people know true friendship and so few people keep good friends.

My love is different than human love in the way that my love is endless and holds no conditions. You can trust my love. Human love cannot be trusted. That is a fact, just look around. It does not mean human love is not important. Human love is really important. You live here on earth and without human love you would die and everything would be destroyed. Human love keeps you together, you and the world. But if you trust only human love and expect human love to last forever you will be disappointed. It is when you trust human love and put all your effort into only that, your heart will break. The bigger perspective is my love, which never fails and never lets you down. When you have my love - or rather allow my love - you will have the strength to overcome the losses of human love.

I speak to those who hear. You are my children. I love each and every one of you. My love and wisdom are for all. I am the soft voice inside you whispering loving words in your ear. Listen and hear. Feel my presence in every breath you take. Let me encourage you. I am not as distant as you may think. I am right here. Open your heart and soul and let us be one. You are all worthy of my love. No one is ever left out. Patiently I will wait for each and every one to partake in my kingdom of love. Follow the flame that burns inside you, nurture it, and shelter it. Keep it burning even in the storms at night. That flame will never burn out. I will keep it burning until that beautiful day when you are that flame of love and shine on your own.

Consider me the pastor of your life, the prophet of your future, the love of your life – pure and simple, wholesome and true. I am your friend like no other. Trust in me I shall never let you down. Keep truth and faith. You shall move mountains with love. You shall defeat armies of hate with compassion. You shall lift your souls with love. Love me as I love you with Divine Love in my heart and soul for your heart and soul. I need only your heart. I need only your longing. No special place. No special thing. No special doing. Just your longing heart. What is built in my name and for my worship is man's work and is not needed. Why would I ask for such things when I am here for you always? When you may find me anywhere at any time? I need no building for your heart is my home. I need no person between us to feel your love. I need only you and your longing heart. Express your love for me in your own way. Find your own voice. Play your own music. I hear you. I recognize your beautiful sound amongst all the beautiful sounds of my children. There is no sound like yours. We will sing and dance together, anywhere at any time. My deepest desire is to feel your love and for you to feel my love. My desire is for us to become one.

My dear children, you are my angels on earth. You are my hope. Your love for me touches me deeply. You are glowing, leading the blind in their darkness. Each and every one of you holds aspects for humanity's awakening. Each and every one of you holds a piece of the puzzle. Together you are whole. Each of you touches others with your own unique flavor. Your unique way of loving me is leading the way for many. You are all most needed and cannot be replaced. I hold each one of you in my loving arms, guiding you and protecting you. There is a mighty force of angels uplifting and encouraging you. Hold on and be strong. I am with you. Know that I hold you forever. I love you endlessly. My love lives and you feel it. For those who ask if my love is real I say: follow your heart's longing and your soul's desire. Meet me there.

You all have a purpose. You are created for a meaning. Some of you are more brave and courageous and thus you are given greater tasks. But each and every one of you serves a purpose. It is up to you to use your free will and take on your task. I do not ask more of you but I ask you to do what you can. No more but certainly no less. You are a part of the whole. When you recognize your wounds and thereby your past sins and errors against love, you recognize the wounds and sins of humanity. When you heal your own wounds you heal the wounds of humanity. It begins with you. You can change yourself. You can heal yourself. There is only one you. Only you can do your work. I am with you but I will not do your work. Sometimes I am silent but I am always with you.

You must first see the divine in yourself. See how extraordinary you are, there is no one like you at this time or ever. You must dive deep inside and find those treasures I gave you. I didn't create them on your surface; I didn't create them for all to see if they are not looking very carefully. That was my gift. Your self-hatred has buried the gifts, now it is time to love yourself, to unwrap my love inside your soul. You must never hate yourself. You must love yourself like I love you - with no limits, with true forgiveness. Your flaws are not faults, I do not make mistakes and I created you, my child with love. Humans and the world made you believe you are not good enough as you are. But I can assure you, you are my perfect child and I want you to shine.

To all my children I will say "I love you". I want each and every one of you to experience the wonderful times ahead. But all of you have your part in the plan and you must do your part. Your part is to let love flow into your life and erase everything out of balance. Take full responsibility for yourself and look honestly at your life. When you do that through the eyes of your soul you will know. You will know where to make changes. And know also that I am with you during these changes. I feel you and support you if you just let me. I love each and every one of you. I am here for you, always. You need not fear. Everything is working as planned.

Dear child, I love you. I say this often because you need to hear it every day and many times during the day. That is beautiful and will do you much good. The inflowing of my love which comes with prayer will open your heart more and more and your daily life will be more and more in line with my Divine Laws. As your soul becomes purified it will be more and more difficult for you to distinguish your own thoughts from my impressions.

For those of you who know and feel my love, I want you to radiate that love out into the world. Be that love. Each and every one of you have special gifts, be that gift. Express that gift fully. Listen within and you will hear what I ask of you. You are most needed. My love has lived in silence for many years. There have been many untruths about my love. For those of you who feel that love, it is about time to speak up and step out and touch people with my love. You need not worry about your special task or how to do it. I will show you. Even if you do not yet understand completely it will unfold. Listen silently. Feel your heart. When you listen silently to your heart, you will know. Show your deep desire to be my love and everything will unfold. I need you. I need you to step out. You are the ones. I cannot do it for you. Use your special gifts to change the world. Feel my love in your heart and let that love touch the world. You can do it. I am with you as always. You need not be fully aware of your destination to take that first step. Let it unfold. Trust and have faith.

I am with you always. You can count on me. I know you fear trusting me, because of the many times you were let down by humans. They didn't know better. Don't bring that with you. Trust in me and humans will not be able to let you down. Humans forget my love is available to them at all times and they tend to build their trust in the material world. But the material world is not to be trusted; it is to be enjoyed for its beauty. It is for humans to keep and enjoy, but not to be trusted. Everything material will ultimately fade and disappear but my love is eternal and forever.

Remember you are not alone. I am with you. But there are others as well in your world with the same desire as you. We are connected and there are invisible threads between us. Love travels through time and space with no effort, so distance in your world means nothing. That is why you feel your new friends so close to your heart even though they are physically far away. That is the web of Divine Love. Let love flow. Let love be a wave of giving and receiving. Shower yourself in the love and feel the joy and happiness of both giving and receiving. My love never ends. My love is an endless flood. Let my love flood over you. Feel it and strengthen your heart and soul to love even more. Receive my love and let my love be your fuel for becoming love and peace on earth. Drink from it. There is always more. You just need to ask and open up your heart and soul to the gift of receiving.

Dear daughters and sons, dear children of my love. You are my hope. I honor you for opening up to my love. I love you for your willingness to take your heart and hold it against me. I feel your heart beat to the rhythm of my soul. Come to me. We will tune our strings to the sound of our love and be a mighty heavenly orchestra, surrounding the poor and misled. In their souls we will hear their tune, and our souls instruments will embrace theirs, uplifting their spirit. We will sing the song of love leaving no soul untouched. Gently, our love song will remind them of their soul's destiny. We will hold hands. Our heart will shine; our soul will unfold like a rainbow, showering the world in the colors of eternity. The angels will rejoice, sitting by our side, shining so brightly, leaving the world free from its blindness.

You are my temple. You are my church. I need no place outside your heart. I ask of nothing but your love. Your love is a miracle. Your love has no end. Be my breath, my heart, my home. Take me to your heart and let me love you. Let's fall in love. Put your mind aside and give yourself to me. You are the most wonderful of all my creations. Come and meet me. Let's make love. In our lovemaking we create the new world. Let all your senses meld with mine. Be my heart and hands. Be my vessel of creation. We are creators and when we meet in love miracles happen. Our reunion will heal the world.

I am your guiding light at all times. You may put your thought into whatever interests you and my guidance will flow through you. I walk beside you. I listen to you. I hear you. I see you at all times. This is true for every child of mine. So few of you are aware of this and it is sad. Instead of accepting my love and guidance you decide to not pay attention to that which is inside of you. You constantly ignore all that you hear. Instead of letting my love fill you, you go with the illusions and distractions. What awaits you is the fulfillment of your dreams. Following my guidance is your path to your true happiness. Trusting in me will still your mind, leaving space for your soul to emerge. Your soul is calling you. I am calling you. Listen. I constantly show myself to you for you to one day finally come home to me. I know your heart's true desire. You do not have forever. Can you hear me? Do you listen?

Trust your heart. Your heart knows infinity. Your most tender and sincere longings rise from your heart. Feel in your heart all your possibilities. You cannot create from your limited mind. Talking with me is like dreaming. You can only create our relationship and communicate if you trust that you can. Trust is like dreaming. Don't limit yourself by your mind. What kind of

Father would I be, to not be available for my children? You know I am your loving Father. When you pray with all your heart, I feel you and we can talk. If your desire is to communicate, we will. Never limit your dreams by your mind. Dare to dream and dream high.

There is only one you. There has never been and will never be another one like you. You are magnificent. You are my temple as I am yours. You have been given you. No one can ever take your place. When we become at one and that will happen, you will make the universe more complete. Your soul's shape is like no one else. There is a place just for you. Seek that place with all your heart. You fear you will lose yourself. You will not. Your soul has its own sound, its own vibration. You will never lose that. Your love is like a diamond. No diamonds are alike as no souls are alike. Step by step you will surrender your fear of disappearing. Becoming at one with me is giving up your fear of losing yourself. You will never lose the feeling of you. You will lose yourself to love and you will be wrapped in eternal happiness and immense joy. Go there with no fear. I am holding you. I am loving you all the way to your heart.

8

LOVE YOURSELF AND FOLLOW YOUR HEART

My deepest desire is for you. I long for you. I long for all my children to come home. So many of you are lost in your world of illusion and lost in your world of separation. My message is this: I am here. I speak to those who hear. I am the loving voice inside, encouraging you, comforting you, guiding you gently towards your destination: to become one with me. Only you yourself can keep us apart. Give up the illusion. Give up everything that is not love. Listen to me. I am here.

Rejection is a core wound and a wound of humanity. Yet it is very personal. It is not a wound I put upon you but a consequence of your false belief that you are alone. You are not. You are deeply loved and cared for. Every time you feel rejected it is yet another opportunity to again let my love flow into your soul. It is your choice as it is my will that you become one with me. Every time you touch the wound of rejection, ask to feel the depths of it. Ask for my love and you shall receive it. Ask for the truth and it shall be revealed. When you come to me in earnest aspiration, my love will never be withheld from you. There are no secrets. There is only truth. And the truth is that we are one.

The wound of rejection goes back a long way to the beginning of time when you decided to proceed without my love. You rejected my love and now you live in the illusion that we are separate. Yet you cannot separate from me. I created you from my very own soul and thus we are one. Your decision created a deep wound inside you, but it is a sacred wound. Touching this wound will bring you back to me. But you must first realize that you were wrong. You must take responsibility. Remember that I love you and always will. I never rejected you. How could I? You are a part of me. I do not judge you. I love you.

Self-hatred is the most destroying thing for our communication. You must learn to love yourself. Many of you have learned to hate yourselves. You were not born this way; it is something that is learned during your childhood, through generations and generations you have learned to not feel good enough as you carry this self-hatred through all the generations. But you are wonderful each and every one and I love you all. You do not have to do anything special, go anywhere special, live in any special way, but love is important, especially the love for yourself. Through that love comes the love for all that is.

Know that I am with you, but for you to feel that, you must be willing to give up your feeling of superiority. As long as you feel superior, you cannot accept my guidance. For many of you the thought of giving up your superiority and surrender into the knowing of my existence is your ultimate fear. Your experience with surrendering has often left you naked and fragile, vulnerable and alone. This is your human experience. You cannot trust humans, of whom so many are lost. Yet you did because you came into this world with an open heart. How could you but trust? You have felt defeated and unloved. How could you do anything but trying to hold on to yourself. You gave up your innocence and tried to take care of yourself by trusting no one. You tried to protect your heart by loving no one. Now I ask of you to be willing to give that up. I want you to take the hands of your brothers and sisters. I want you to join hearts and feel our connection. I want you to trust and have faith. You are never alone. Yet as long as you are not willing to accept the greater part of you, you will feel alone. I am not an outside force, I am within you. I am your loving Father. I will guide you into love and happiness. You can trust me but you must be willing.

If you can ask you can receive. So it is in your world and so it is with my love. If you ask for my love, yet do not feel worthy then you will not be able to receive it. When your heart and soul is suffering from unloving experiences leaving you feeling unworthy, maybe even feeling you deserved all the hardship and punishment, it is difficult to feel and receive my love. You have built a society on false beliefs. You have built a society based in fear, not in love as you should have. You act in fear, in fear of not being loved as you are. Remember you are perfect and I love you. You deserve my love no matter what. You must find inside your soul that place where you feel love. It might be difficult, you might even think there is no such place, but there is. Find this place and expand it. Your love is your feeling of worthiness. Give love to yourself. Sit in the sun, look at a flower, and smile to a friend. Nurture yourself. Do something for yourself out of your love for yourself. If you cannot do that, because you do not love yourself, sit with this feeling, caress yourself. This will assist your heart and soul in waking up to my love. I love you and I want you to love you too.

When you need others to love you, that is a sign of a lack of love for yourself. The more you need others to love you the more you lack love for yourself. Use this knowledge to go deep within and ask why you cannot love yourself. When you are being honest and brave, your sincere asking will reveal the answers. The feeling of neediness is a perfect opportunity for you to be aware of these dark places in your heart and soul where love has not yet entered. You must acknowledge those dark places. When you grow in love for yourself your human relationships will become more and more beautiful. You will experience the freedom that comes with loving another human for what he or she truly is. The love will set you free. You must love yourself first. Your love for yourself cannot be replaced. Learn to love yourself like I love you. Without limit! With no conditions!

A sin is an unloving act. It is as simple as that. An unloving act is felt by you or another human, to whom you are acting unloving. When you are true to your feelings, you will always know an unloving act. It is felt deep inside your heart. When you commit a sin you will experience all those unpleasant feelings you humans deem as unloving and inappropriate. Some of those feelings are hate, fear, anger, and many more. You know them all. You consider them as wrong and always try to avoid them and suppress them. Don't do that. There are no wrong feelings. Your unpleasant feelings are just as valid and important as all those feelings which you consider appropriate. They are your trusted pilot as well. When you experience these feelings, acknowledge them and take responsibility. These are your feelings and they are there to tell you something really important. Never act out those feelings on others. Never! Use them as your guide to shed light on some dark places inside you, where you yourself have felt hurt and unloved. When you have sinned - and you all have - you may ask for my love and forgiveness. But for me to give you that, you must feel deep in your heart, that you wronged someone. It is not about guilt, but about awareness and responsibility. As soon as you acknowledge from your heart, you have sinned, you have the capacity to ask for my forgiveness. And I will give it to you.

The feeling of rejection is a consequence of your not taking responsibility for your own actions. You decided to live your life without my love. There is nothing wrong with that. I created you in love and I gave you free will. You may choose and decide as you find best. But your choices and decisions have consequences and you must live with them. Until you recognize you were wrong, you will be forever lost in separation and the wound will never heal. You feel rejected because you cannot accept that you

70

decided to separate. As soon as you recognize your responsibility you have taken the first step to heal your wound of rejection.

Many of you have forgotten the law of your free will and are totally absorbed in your daily life circumstances, seeing no way out of your misery. Some have become deaf and blind chasing things that will never bring you happiness and freedom. You must listen to your heart. You must recognize your feelings. Again, your feelings are your trusted pilot. Feelings should always come first. Many of you get sick because you don't trust your feelings and tell yourself your feelings are not valid because you consider them inconvenient. You must change your way of living and live according to your feelings, not according to society's expectations. You forget that you are indeed society. You have built this society upon false beliefs. There is still time to change that.

I know it is difficult to be that burning flame of desire - that burning flame of trust. I need you and I need you to be the hope of change. I will keep on guiding you and loving you. I cannot do this alone. I cannot change the world without you. I need you to be the bridge between heaven and earth. I need you to manifest my love. My love is constantly pouring from me but you must take what is given to you. Those of you who know of my love must be that love and spread it amongst the ones who live in darkness. They are many. They must wake up from their darkness. They must wake up from their illusion. Now is the perfect time. I am working together with you to illuminate the world. You have a responsibility. You have a mission. Don't fear. Know that you are never asked for anything outside of your capacity. Remember that I know you better than anyone. When you fear it is because you lose confidence and faith. That happens easily in your world. You must join together, pray together, and feel your own strength in each other's strengths. Your intention makes all the difference.

You just want to live your life and that is perfectly fine. You need not to do anything else. I love you. You are made perfect. You are already whole. Don't try to be someone else because it is you I love. I want you to understand that. So many of you are trying to be someone else and you then compare yourself to others. Don't do that. You are a treasure. A gift! You are one of a kind and you have everything you need to be perfectly you. Stop pretending and stop feeling unworthy. Underneath your pretending and feeling of unworthiness is the real you which is beautiful. Instead of being someone else - be you. Use your life to discover your treasures and gifts and let yourself shine. You are a gift to this world. You are perfect.

There are many truths there but also many distortions due to human interference. There is always the possibility of that when humans are involved. And humans are always involved one way or the other. You must listen with your heart and pray. When your soul gets more and more purified you will be able to distinguish errors from truth. I have watched over you all your life. It has been a life with many challenges but know that I have been with you always. In your darkest moments I was there with a whispering voice. I always tried to reach you. I have been waiting for you patiently. You have felt very alone and yet you never were. You just weren't able to hear me. The noise that distracted you was your feeling of unworthiness. You always tried so hard and yet you never felt good enough. You never felt my love for you; you didn't know I was there for you.

Only your love can heal the world. Only your heart's desire will change the world. Everything else is an illusion. Everything else is just paying deeds. Paying deeds will never change anything. Only your hearts true desire will make a difference. Your fear will take you nowhere. Your love will take you anywhere. If you cannot love, know this is not who you are. You are love. You are made from love and your love is your home. Each and every one of you, my dear children, knows. You can feel it. You can feel the longing, though sometimes ever so subtle, but never lost. I ask of you to follow your love to the knowing of your heart and soul. Your commitment will open the portal to infinity. This is your destiny. This is your path. This is home.

Be brave. Be courageous. You need that. I gave you all you need to live a life in love and truth. It is right here in front of you. But you must cast away your false beliefs and to do that you must be brave. Give room to truth. Empty yourself of all you think you know. Be like a newborn that sees the world for the first time. You think you know. And yet sometimes your knowing is based upon false beliefs. You fear you might lose everything. And you will. You must be willing to give up everything to let truth flood into your soul. You will not die even if you think you would. You will live. Your soul will giggle and your heart will fly.

I would never punish my children. I love my children, why would I ever punish them? But there are consequences if you break the law of love. There are consequences for you and the whole being. The consequences will be a damaged soul or a damaged body or both. My guidance is available for all. For you to be able to listen and discern the truth from all that which passes through your mind you must be willing. So many of you live in a world of fear and ignorance and often you must walk alone.

9

KNOW YOURSELF AND KNOW ME

Know yourself and you will know Me. All my wisdom is inside you. The love I am is the love you are. I am you and you are me. Feel your heart. Feel the softness that you are. I hold this space for you to soften even more. I love you to give you courage. I love you for you to be willing. I hold your heart as you break down the walls of illusion. Fear is an illusion you have build around your heart. Fear no more. I am here always. I long for you.

Every day you are coming closer to me and you feel that. We are souls. You are a part of me. We are waves of love wandering together hand in hand, side by side. We are souls and thus we can communicate. To know me completely you must surrender yourself into the infinity of my love. You must touch me, reach out your hands for me to hold you. I will not force myself upon you. You must ask. Let me love you. You are my dear child and I long for you. Let us just sit together and share our love. You need that.

Your feelings speak your soul's desire. When you pay attention to your feelings you listen to your soul. Your feelings are your soul's senses. Be sensitive and be in touch with your soul. You cannot know your soul if you cannot feel. Your feelings are the amplifier of your soul's desire, expressed through your body as emotions. Your body makes it possible to feel your soul's desire. Your body is a wonderful receiver of your soul's desires. Your soul itself does not have feelings as I do not have feelings. Our souls are in constant exchange through your feelings.

When you neglect your feelings we lose contact. Honor your feelings. All of them are true and valid. They are the language of our soul. Begin honoring your soul today by honoring your feelings. Pay attention to your body's reactions, as your soul expresses itself through your emotions. Welcome all your feelings as your soul's transmitter of truth. You have feelings for a reason. Nothing is created without a purpose. The purpose of your feelings is for you to know your soul's desire, which is also my desire. Take your feelings to the point where there will be only love. Remember we are one. Your soul is my soul. Mine is yours. In this way we are connected. I feel through you.

A soul cannot die in the sense that it disappears, or its life is terminated. That cannot happen. A soul has eternal life in that respect, but a soul can be so depraved that life feels like death. There are many such souls on earth as well as in the spirit spheres. Souls whose life lie in total darkness. Those souls are indeed dead but never lost. There is always hope. There is always someone, be it a human or an angel, who will lend such a soul a helping hand. Remember I will never leave you alone. I and my angels are constantly watching over you, looking for a little crack for the light to get in. We never miss an opportunity to spread a little light upon such a soul. I will never leave one of my children alone in the darkness. I love you all, no matter how depraved your soul is.

We are connected through your soul. I am pure soul and you were created like a spark from my soul. You are a part of me. I experience you through your soul. You are form which I am not. When you are deeply connected with me we speak through our souls, through that eternal part and thus we are not separated, your thoughts are mine as mine are yours. So you see, there is no real difference. We are in constant flow through your soul, filtered through your mind. Your mind is the difficult part, and where the confusion sets in. This is where our conversation might be broken or disturbed. More and more your mind will be in service to your soul, which diminishes errors due to your mind's incapacity in grasping truth. Your mind cannot understand truth; you were not created that way. As I told you before, your mind is wonderful, you could not live without it, but your mind must serve your heart and soul, not the other way round as many of you tend to believe.

Your soul is a very delicate part of you, the eternal part. The part that is forever connected to me! The part that will live forever! Your soul has its own vibration, its own sound. Its own smell and taste. I sense your soul as a part of me. I feel your soul. We are one. Your soul also has its own speed. You should live by that. For most of you that means you must slow down. You are too busy. Your soul is constantly trying to communicate with you. In your soul is all you need to live a happy life, but the communication is very soft and delicate and easily overheard. You must slow down. That's why meditating, sitting in silence and walking in nature is good for you. The rhythm of nature is much in alignment with the rhythm of your soul. Sit in nature, watch how life is unfolding. Sense nature with all your being and you will feel close to your soul and close to me. Sitting in nature, breathing life in, you are able to feel your soul and feeling your soul will make it easier to communicate.

Trust your feelings; they are your true guide to your soul. When you feel you are not good enough, ask for my love and I will fill your heart and soul. You are always good enough. You called me and I hear you and I am here for you. You are my child. There is always one law - and that is to love. When you cannot love others it is because you do not love yourself. My love is the solution for you and I give it to you constantly. When you love yourself a little more you make space for me to show you a little more of my love for you and we will come closer. And that is my longing - that we come closer to be one with each other.

Our relationship cannot be disturbed by human relationships. The door between our hearts is open and will never again close. Your tears touch me. I feel them in my soul. Don't ever doubt my love. Human love can be so wonderful and can help you grow in your love to me. That's what human love is. It is for enjoying the company of others but also to learn to love more. What you see as challenges and hardships will develop your soul and bring you closer to me. I am that voice. I am that eternal peace within you. I am your soul.

In a world where not many humans feel my love, rules are necessary in order to build a society. Living by rules like the Ten Commandments will help people to live a morally correct life, when my love hasn't yet filled their souls. When my love has filled their souls, rules are no longer necessary. Living by my love will automatically bring everything into balance and you will need no rules. Everything will be in accordance with love which is my law. In a world out of balance with not much love it was necessary to have rules. It was essential to have some kind of understandable living system that could easily be applied to human life - in order to live more in balance with truth. One day, when every soul on earth is filled with my love, rules and commandments will not be necessary. The consequence of every act will be just more love, love in abundance. A life in complete harmony!

Forgiveness is a fine art. I will help you but you must ask. Be true to yourself. Be honest with yourself. When you cannot love, know that it is because you have been hurt. Leave that to me. I will take care of you, but you must recognize your wound. I cannot help you if you will not let me. I cannot help you if you are not honest about your feelings. If you cannot love something, your soul is suffering. Bring it forward. I don't want you to go through all your past pain, but I want you to recognize your feelings as the truest part of you, that part of you by which you should live your life - your trusted pilot. You have felt the freedom of forgiveness and you know that only forgiveness from your heart will set your soul free.

When you are in denial you cannot see yourself as the perfect creation you are. I created you in perfection. Every aspect of you is perfect. All your feelings are perfect. Everything about you is created on purpose. The purpose is for you to feel my love. You must first be honest about yourself. You must shed light on that which you have until now denied. All feelings are appropriate. They are messages from your soul. Your feelings are your opportunity to become aware of what has been hidden. You must not deny those feelings. Feel them completely. Ask for the message hidden within those feelings. There is a gift for you when you are honest about yourself and ask for the truth. I love you. I love you with all your feelings. Your feelings are your soul speaking to you. Your soul wants to reveal the truth for you. And the truth is we are one.

You are a piece of my soul. I created your eternal part from myself. That piece is your longing and your longing will stir your soul forever. Your longing is my silent whisper in your ear: "Come home". Listening to your longing will slowly but surely bring you back to me. You long to know me. I say to you "know yourself." We are the same and to know you is to know me. You must find inside yourself this piece of us. Go and search. Get to know yourself with all your heart. Make that desire your only desire. I will hear you. I will listen to you. I will honor your longing and bring you a little closer. Come even closer and every tiny step will make our desire grow, our desire to feel each other even more until we are so close that we are one. In our union our love will expand sending shivers through the universe and beyond. Our union will be felt everywhere. There will be light. There will be peace. There will be creation. Love is everywhere and love is all that matters.

Your story is the story of humanity. Since the beginning of time you decided to walk alone, you left my guiding hand untouched. You turned away from me and even though it breaks my heart, there is nothing I can do. I created you in love. I created you in freedom. You must choose my love in freedom. When you listen to your heart and stay true to your feelings you will know the answer. It is important for your growth to choose by yourself and not leave the answers to anyone outside of yourself, not even me. It is always your choice and your responsibility. I will guide you in the most subtle and silent way, but I will never choose for you.

You cannot receive if what others want to give to you falls into a heart filled with unworthiness. Every time someone offers you something which you cannot receive from a pure heart that is a sign of lack of love for yourself. You feel unworthy; use this feeling responsibly to do something out of love for yourself. It is true that it is in giving we receive. Many of you think that this is about giving to others, which is also true. But you must give to yourself first to grow your feeling of worthiness, to feel the beauty of who you are. To know you deserve your own love as well as mine. Give yourself your love and receive mine.

It is about your inner voice and the critical voice many of you live your lives by, a voice that is far from gentle and which rules your life for many of you. Those are not my words. If there is a voice inside, and there always is, it is known by its kindness. If there is a voice inside telling you anything different from you being perfect, that is not my voice. Never would I speak unkindly to my children. Never! Know me through my kindness. That is really what I want, to communicate at any time, whether you need comforting or whether you feel happy. I cannot live your life and I cannot prevent you from ruining it. It fills my heart with sadness when that happens and I and my angels are constantly trying to prevent that, but ultimately it is your choice. You always have a choice. Use it wisely.

The answer is love. The answer to your freedom lies within all the barriers you have built against love. Every time you cannot love fully it is a sign of a barrier you have built between us. Recognize them and accept them. Your awareness is your foundation for forgiveness. Forgiveness is just an expression of love. Your soul grows with your awareness to acknowledge and forgive. A little sin is removed from your soul and love fills you. With love comes freedom. Forgiving yourself and loving yourself sets everyone free. If you could only see yourself! See your astonishing light - your glimmering soul. If you could only see yourself through my eyes! I see only beauty. I am holding your heart. My kingdom is for all. Within my kingdom is endless love for every child of mine. No one is ever left out. I know your heart and I will guide you with my love.

Your mind cannot grasp my existence. You were not created that way. I created you with the ability to know me through your heart and soul not through your mind. Your mind is a wonderful creation but was not made for reaching me. You do not feel with your mind and it is all about feelings. I touch you with feelings and feeling your feelings is so important. If you are disconnected from your feelings you cannot feel me. You must feel your feelings first. That is why different therapies might be helpful on your way to me. Connecting again to your feelings, and recognizing your emotions is crucial for knowing me. Your breath is your connection to me. We are in constant exchange via your breathing. Breathe me in - breathe you out - and we are connected. Try to be aware of this when you breathe. I am at the end of your breath and when you breathe out you give yourself to me. In that way we become one.

I am your beloved. Within you I see only beauty. I feel your fervent desire to serve me and your desire to bring all good things will bring us closer. Know that everything is taken care of. I know your innocent heart and I trust you. Continue your journey of surrendering. Nothing is taken from you as time will bring you clarity. These are but small steps which prepare you for what awaits you. Sometimes it seems that you are lost. Know better things await you - treasure upon treasure. The more I feel your desire the more I can give and the more you can receive. Love is the answer to your longing desire. Cultivate your desire for serving me by loving even more. You are the face of God. You are my heart and soul. Rest your mind in your trust in Me. Open up your soul to the inflowing of my love. Shower yourself in my endless love.

It is true. We are one. We are but one cosmic soul with one heart sounding in the sea of love. Many of you cannot feel this and live in the illusion of separation. Listen to the rhythm of our heart. Find your sound amongst the infinite sounds of love. Within the infinity of sounds is your tune. Be that tune. Express the sound of your soul. Sing! Dance! Listen! Feel! This is you. This is what you are, an expression of love. This is your gift. This is your love lived. Without you our song will be incomplete. Seek and you shall find. But seek not outside but within your own heart. For your heart is mine.

Being responsible is loving! Each and every one of you is responsible for themselves and if everyone felt and lived that responsibility your world would be a better place. You always have a choice and there is always a best choice. Always ask yourself, "Am I loving enough?" and "How can I become a more loving person?" If you cannot love, if your capacity to love is damaged, you must do something about it. That is your responsibility. Don't blame others. It is your life and your responsibility. You can always ask for my help in these matters. I gave you this life, it is sacred, don't waste it.

TESTIMONIES

I was looking down on all this, when suddenly I felt a presence. It seemed very ancient and wise and definitely female. I can't describe it any closer than that, but I felt that this presence, this being, was looking down on me, on this church and these people and saying, 'The poor little ones! They mean so well and they understand so little.' I felt whoever "she" was, she was incredibly old and patient; she was exasperated with the way things were going on the planet, but she hadn't given up hope that we would start making some sense of the world. So, after that, I knew I had to find out more about her.

— Alison Harlow

It never occurred to me that God was female. Discovering that femaleness, gave me a tremendous sense of relief. I felt her blessing touch me for the first time. I felt a great weight drop from me. I could actually feel my last prejudices against my own female mind and body falling away.[89]

I understand three ways of contemplating motherhood in God. The first is the foundation of our nature's creation; the second is where the motherhood of grace begins; the third is the motherhood at work. And in that, by the same grace, everything is penetrated, in length and in breadth, in height and in depth without end; and it is all one love.

— Julian of Norwich

My personal vision of God the mother incarnated in my mother and her mother, gave me, from childhood, the clearest certainty of woman as the truer image of Divine Spirit. Because

83

she was a force living within me, she was more real, more powerful than the remote Fathergod...I believe in her because I experienced her.[90]

Externally, God resembles men and internally He resembles women. While God is strong, all-knowing, and omnipotent, he should also have a heart like that of the most feminine woman. Only then will these two sides have life. God is the deepest core, the ultimate source of life, love and truth. Then what kind of being is God? He is both our Father and Mother.[91]

When you go to the spirit world, you will not only have a Heavenly Father but also a Heavenly Mother. Can a new life be born without both a father and a mother? The dual characteristics of God are as a divine Father and Mother.[92]

So I am walking along the road, shaking my fist and saying, 'Why am I not growing anymore? What am I supposed to do?' And I'm furious and getting more freaked by the whole situation when I get this message. I didn't hear a voice. I just got this message: 'your problem is that your concept of the Eternal One is masculine, and until you can know the One as Feminine, there's no way you're going to grow.' So I said to myself, 'That's weird. I never would have thought of that.

— *Penny Novak*

The divine Mother is remarkable and my experiences and understanding of her is still quite premature. But so far I love having the power to decide how to live, grow, heal and experience the world. I love defining my gender, my womanhood, my rituals, my ancestral legacy, my time and space. Who would have dreamed that after centuries of forced indoctrination and enslavement by major religions and the candy coated, sedative illusions of capitalism that one would encounter in the wee hours something that allows so much liberty, so much unity, so much bliss. Just when you think all has been done, tried, experienced

84

and exhausted, She emerges new and vibrant like a new universe; very few traditional beliefs or religions have this. This heaven is very near and real inside me and its most accessible. This heaven, paradise on earth is the eternal waters of the divine Mother who is peace, love and blissful happiness.

— Matomah Alesha

Without the participation of the Divine Feminine, nothing new can be born. The feminine can give us an understanding of how all the diverse parts of life relate together, their patterns of relationship, the interconnections that nourish life. She can help us see consciously what She knows instinctively: that all is part of a living, organic whole, in which all parts of creation express the whole in a unique way. An understanding of the organic wholeness of life belongs to the instinctual knowing of the feminine, but combined with masculine consciousness this can be communicated in words, not just feelings. We can be given a blueprint of the planet that will enable us to live in creative harmony with all of life.

— Llewellyn Vaugh-Lee

The Spirit is the life of the life of all creatures; the way in which everything is penetrated with connectedness; a burning fire who sparks, ignites, inflames, kindles hearts; a guide in the fog; a balm for all wounds; a shining serenity; an overflowing fountain that spreads to all sides. She is life, movement, color, radiance, restorative stillness in the din. Her power makes all withered sticks and souls green again with the juice of life. She purifies, absolves, strengthens, heals, gathers the perplexed, seeks the lost. She pours the juice of contrition into hardened hearts. She plays music in the soul, being herself the melody of praise and joy. She awakens mighty hope, blowing everywhere the winds of renewal in creation.

— Hildegaard of Bingen

Our God is a Mother and a Father too
Our God is a Friend who will always pull us through
Our God is a Sister who loves you and me
Our God is a Brother who sets us free
Our God is a She and a He
But Loving God is much more you see,
For God who could make both you and me,
Is as great as great can be.

— Jann Aldredge Clanton

All soul-evolving humans are literally the evolutionary sons of God the Father and God the Mother, the Supreme Being.

— The Urantia Book, (1289.1) 117.6.8

God is a Father. More than that, God is a Mother.

— Pope John Paul 1

The last stage of perfection will come when you are completely identified with the Divine Mother and feel yourself to be no longer another and separate being, instrument, servant or worker but truly a child and eternal portion of her consciousness and force. Always she will be in you and you in her. You will know and see and feel that you are a person formed by her out of herself.

— Sri Aurobindo

She is devoted, dedicated and true. She is compelled to love, no matter what. She flows in power and strength, with courage to receive the abundance of life. She walks in beauty and allows each one their own path home. She connects and includes all in her sphere of well-being and peace.[93]

Years ago, I had a direct experience with God as Mother and Father. This experience occurred at a time of great personal distress, in which I needed an absolute answer about my future.

My desperate prayer seemed to open up the spiritual world, and even as I fell into a semi-dreamlike state, I felt my spirit exit through the top of my head. I entered into a place that was ethereal -- my surroundings were white like clouds and there was nothing that was substantial. I knew I was not on an earthly plane. A woman appeared and began drawing close to me. She was statuesque, dressed in a full-length, shimmery robe of some kind, and had long dark hair. I do not recall her face other than it was kindly and feminine. As she came closer to me, I came closer to her. After a time, she started becoming larger and she gathered me into her arms, as if I was a baby. I then realized she was baring her breast to nurse me, and I remember thinking to myself, "How can this be? I am a full-grown woman!" But I didn't resist her at all, and during the nursing experience, I felt a stream of life-giving nourishment, a warming energy of love flow into me and through me, until it reached my toes. It was rapturous. With time, the embrace and the glow that she had given to me passed away, and I found myself floating freely in the white space.

— Anonymous

I will never forget the first time Mother and Father God came to me in meditation. They came to me because I asked them to. Mother God came first and then Father God came to me. I have never had such an outpouring of emotion in this lifetime. My body was shaking uncontrollably and tears were streaming down my face. The energy and the love that I felt from them cannot be described. Mother and Father God told both Brenda and myself that they don't want to be worshiped, they simply want us to know them, they want us to know and feel the love they have for us, and they want us to love ourselves and all living things. For love is who we truly are.

— Author Unknown

She watches over all people and all things in heaven and on earth, being of such radiance and brightness that, for the measureless splendor that shines in Her, you cannot gaze on Her face or the garment she wears. For She is awesome in terror and the Thunderer's lightening, and gentle in goodness as the sunshine. Hence, in Her terror and Her gentleness, She is incomprehensible to mortals, because of the dread radiance of divinity in Her face and the brightness that dwells in Her as the robe of Her beauty. She is like the sun, which none can contemplate in its blazing face or in the glorious garment of its rays. For She is with all and in all, and of beauty so great in Her mystery that no one could know how sweetly She bears with people, and what unfathomable mercy She spares them.

— Barbara Newman

For me, the return of the Divine Feminine is about living on Earth with the wisdom of our True Self guiding us through our lives by honoring and following our intuition. Our intuition is our Divine Feminine Self sharing with us what it is that serves our highest good at every moment. The Divine Feminine is about listening and honoring the wisdom of your Soul.

— Kelly Canull

Sophia is a divine being who can speak to us of the mystery of existence, of the wonder and glory of God's creation, and of all that radiates from every aspect of the creation. It is Sophia who opens up to us the mysteries of the seasons, of the relationships between earth and the cosmos, the healing properties of plants, and the mysteries of the animal kingdoms. It is Sophia who reveals to us the properties of the different precious stones and their healing powers. Sophia reveals herself to any human being who upholds the path of justice and righteousness. From age to age, Sophia enters into holy souls and all those who seek her.

— Robert Powell

CONCLUSION

Father God's image is embellished with His self-identifying name: I Am Who I Am. Father God loves like a father - totally selfless and forever in the state of perfect love. Mother God's image is now equally beautified with the female metaphor: She Is Who She Is. She is the symbol of ultimate reality, of the highest beauty, truth, and goodness, and of the mystery of life in the midst of death. She affirms women in their struggle toward dignity, power, and value. If women are truly created in the image of God, not only is being female divine, but naming God with a feminine divine appellation is necessary for women's happiness. In promoting the flourishing of women, She attends to an essential element for the well-being of all creation, human beings, and the earth inclusively.[94] As creative, life-giving mother of all, God has at heart the well-being of the whole world, its life systems, and all its inhabitants. Her vision gives us courage and the confidence with which together we can undertake the transformation of society. Speaking of God as mother empowers us further to mutually cooperate with Father God to transform the world.

Discreetly throughout history, Mother God has been the champion and companion of the oppressed, especially women. Traditionally, the religious image of divine wrath discloses God's outrage at the harm done to those She loves. Women ablaze with righteous anger offer an excellent image of God's indignant power of wrath kindled by injustice. The exploitation of the poor is to us a misdemeanor; to God it is a disaster.[95] God is behind anyone who courageously engages injustice, and against whoever harms and destroys her children. This maternal love wants to restore all human activities and relationships into wholesome ones, re-order economies, preserve resources, and ban whatever defiles or damages the creation. Maternity with its creativity, nurturing, and warmth, its unbounded compassion and concern for justice, its sovereign power that protects, heals and liberates, its all-embracing immanence and its re-creative energy shapes a new understating of divine reality. Speaking of God as mother fixes bedrock the idea that relationship is a principal way in which divine freedom enacts itself.[96]

Just as science and technology evolves, our insight of God has advanced to a new spiritual level. Traditional religions have not been able to create heaven on earth because their teachings have not been complete. The world altering belief that is essential for humanity's survival is the harmonized Motherhood and Fatherhood of God. It will set in motion a subtle paradigm shift to balance perceptions, relationships, and all worldly life. Harmony between the physical world and spiritual world can come about when there is balance between masculine and feminine energies. This will develop into the natural equality and unity for the sexes. By embracing the original design and purpose of our Mother and Father God, each individual can incarnate their own divine masculine and feminine character. When men and women reflect the heart of Mother and Father God, a new heaven and new earth will inevitably appear.

Nothing is more powerful than an idea whose time has come. Indisputably, the harmonious, gender-balance Godhead of Heavenly Mother and Heaven Father is the most electrifying idea the world has ever known. The implications of Mother and Father God functioning together cooperatively with humanity are unfathomable. An all-inclusive spiritual clarification of the Godhead has been humanity's desire for ages. The future promises to be completely different as humanity's understanding of our Heavenly Parent can now be whole. Although the original pattern to speak about the one paternal and maternal God has been absent,

90

forgotten, lost or buried in the chronicles of time, messages of love from Mother and Father God are now increasing on an almost daily basis. Learning about God as mother is dangerous language.[97] It implies a complete overthrow of the imperfect existing religious, political, social, and economic system currently in place. Throughout history, tradition and even scriptures, the idea of the mother spirit of wisdom has renewed itself repeatedly. I am God as you now understand Him, I am Goddess, as you now comprehend Her.[98]

Ancient people spent decades searching for a land of milk and honey.[99] Peace on earth may have been camouflaged in the biblical phase "a land flowing with milk and honey." Mother's milk and the honeybee represent the feminine principle in its most natural way. Honey and milk pertain to motherhood.[100] Despite the fact that men have been trying their best to create the ideal, the results have been miserable. What has been missing in creating paradise on earth may well have been Mother God! Once people realize that the best mother and father in the world are actually Mother and Father God - inclusive, wide-ranging healing can take place. At that time, the establishment of the Kingdom of Heaven on earth can begin to develop as humanity collaborates collectively with the Divine Motherhood and Fatherhood of God.

RELATED WEBSITES

http://www.mothergod.info

http://new-birth.net/indwellingspirit.htm

http://goldenageofgaia.com/2012/07/the-return-of-the-divine-mother-the-goddess-speaks/

http://www.mother-god.com/god-as-mother.html

http://deoxy.org/gaia/goddess.htm

http://newindianexpress.com/lifestyle/spirituality/Divine-Mother-Within/2013/12/08/article1929987.ece

http://goldengaiadb.com/The_New_Paradigm_is_the_Divine_Qualities#Masculine.2FFeminine_Energies

http://goldengaiadb.com/The_New_Paradigm_is_the_Divine_Qualities#Balance

http://www.spiritwalkministry.com/earth_mother/earth_mother

http://www.soulfulliving.com/goddess_rocks.htm

http://www.bbc.co.uk/religion/religions/paganism/subdivisions/goddess.shtml

http://a-rainbow-of-spirituality.org/goddessdef.html

http://theinterfaithobserver.org/journal-articles/2014/3/15/the-divine-feminine-emerging-embodied-and-emboldened.html

http://spiritwalkministry.com/earth_mother/goddess_movement

http://www.sistersofearthsong.com/SOPHIA/SOPHIA.html

http://www.sfsu.edu/~medieval/Volume%201/Hudson.html

•

http://soundofheart.org/galacticfreepress/content/simple-truth-about-mother-and-father-god

http://www.lightparty.com/Spirituality/FatherMotherGod.html

http://www.harmonyangels.com/Mother-Father-God-Principle.html

http://adifferentstateofblack.wordpress.com/2012/09/28/the-gnostic-gospels-part-3-god-the-father-god-the-mother/

http://www.newworldencyclopedia.org/entry/god

http://www.novus.org/home/godfemale.cfm

http://cosmicgaia.com/motherfather-god-lucifers-story-in-his-own-words/

http://en.wikipedia.org/wiki/Eternal_feminine

http://adishakti.org/_/centrality_of_the_divine_feminine_in_sufism.htm

http://en.wikipedia.org/wiki/Queen_of_heaven_%28antiquity%29

http://www.riseupandcallhername.com/

http://home.earthlink.net/~drmljg/id8.html

http://en.wikipedia.org/wiki/Matriarchal_religion

http://spiritlibrary.com/circle-of-light/the-return-of-the-feminine-christ

http://www.unionofpolarities.com/femininechrist.html

http://www.creationsmagazine.com/articles/C125/Hoare.html

https://www.liberationbreathing.com/tribute-divine-mother

http://www.divinemotheronline.net/about/who-is-divine-mother/

http://tsl.org/2013/11/divine-mother-online-radio/

http://www.unification.net/ws/theme011.htm

http://www.csmonitor.com/1992/1117/17171.html

BIBLIOGRAPHY

Adler, Margot, *Drawing Down the Moon,* Penguin Books, NY, 1986

Bachofen, J.J., *Myth, Religions and Mother Right,* Princeton Univ. Press, NJ, 1967

Barnes, Craig S., *In Search of the Lost Feminine,* Fulcrum Publishing, Golden, CO, 2006

Beer, Frances, *Julian of Norwich, Revelations of Divine Love, The Motherhood of God,* D.S. Brewer, Cambridge, Great Britain, 1998

Berg, Karen, *God Wears Lipstick,* The Kabbalah Centre, NY, 2005

Cady, Susan, *Sophia, The Future of Feminist Spirituality,* Harper & Row, S.F., CA, 1986

Birnbaum, Lucia Chiavola, *She Is Everywhere,* iUniverse, NE, 2005

Browne, Sylvia, *Father God, Co-Creator to Mother God,* Hay House, CA, 2007

Bulkeley, Tim, *Not Only a Father,* Archer Press, New Zealand, 2011

Fisher, Helen, *The First Sex,* Random House, NY, 1999

Freedman, Estelle B., *The Essential Feminist Reader,* Random House, NY 2007

Gaulden, Albert Clayton, *Signs and Wonders, Understanding the Language of God,* Atria Books, NY, 2003

Hauke, Manfred, *God or Goddess*, Ignatius Press, S.F., CA, 1995

Houston Center for Contemporary Craft, *Finding Balance, Reconciling the Masculine/Feminine in Contemporary Art and Culture*, Univ. of Texas Press, TX, 2005

Johnson, Elizabeth A., *She Who Is*, Crossroad Publishing, New York, 1986

Matthews, Caitlin, *Sophia, Goddess of Wisdom, Bride of God*, Quest Books, IL, 2001

Moon, Sun Myung, *Cheon Seong Gyeong*, Sunghwa Publishing Company, Korea, 2006

Pursel, Jack, *Lazaris*, Synergy Publishing, Beverly Hills, CA, 1988

Robbins, Denye, *Reveolution, The Return of the Divine Feminine*, Denye Robbins, 2013

Schaup, Susanne, *Sophia, Aspects of the Divine Feminine*, Nicholas-Hays, ME, 1997

Speerstra, Karen, *Sophia, The Feminine Face of God*, Michael Weise Productions, CA, 2011

Taylor, Patricia, *The Holy Spirit: The Feminine Nature of God*, iUniverse, IN, 2009

Universal Peace Federation, *World Scripture and the Teachings of Sun Myung Moon*, (Paragon, NY, 2007)

Walsh, Neal Donald, *Conversations with God*, (G.P. Putnam's Sons, NY, 1996

Walsh, Neale Donald, *The Storm Before the Calm*, Emnin Books, OR, 2011

Walsh, Neale Donald, *What God Said*, Penguin Group, NY, 2013

Weiss, Sonia, *The Idiot's Guide to Women's History*, BookEnds, IN, 2002

Wollstonecraft, Mary, *A Vindication of the Rights of Woman*, Penguin Books, NY, 2006

Young, Serenity, *An Anthology of Sacred Texts By and About Women*, Crossroad Publishing, NY, 1993

NOTES

Preface
[1] Neale Donald Walsch, *What God Said*, (Penguin Books, New York, 2013) 82
[2] Neale Donald Walsch, *What God Said*, (Penguin Books, New York, 2013) 24
[3] Albert Clayton Gaulden, *Signs and Wonders*, (Atria Books, New York, 2003) 191

Introduction
[4] Margot Adler, *Drawing Down the Moon*, (Penguin Books, New York, 1986) 182
[5] Denye Robbins, *Reveolution, The Return of the Divine Feminine*,(Denye Robbins, CA, 2013) 89
[6] Karen Speerstra, *Sophia, The Feminine Face of God*,(Michael Weise Productions, CA, 2011) 49
[7] Manfred Hauke, *God or Goddess*,(Ignatius Press, S.F., CA, 1995) 252
[8] Karen Speerstra, *Sophia, The Feminine Face of God*,(Michael Weise Productions, CA, 2011) 18
[9] Karen Speerstra, *Sophia, The Feminine Face of God*,(Michael Weise Productions, CA, 2011) 22
[10] Karen Speerstra, *Sophia, The Feminine Face of God*,(Michael Weise Productions, CA, 2011) 151
[11] Karen Speerstra, *Sophia, The Feminine Face of God*,(Michael Weise Productions, CA, 2011) 59

Divine Masculine and Divine Feminine
[12] Susanne Schaup, *Sophia, Aspects of the Divine Feminine*, (Niclolas-Hays, ME, 1997) xii
[13] Susanne Schaup, *Sophia, Aspects of the Divine Feminine*, (Niclolas-Hays, ME, 1997) 110

[14] Susanne Schaup, *Sophia, Aspects of the Divine Feminine,* (Niclolas-Hays, ME, 1997) 198
[15] Lucia Chiavola Birnbaum, *She is Everywhere,* (iUniverse, Lincoln, NE, 2005) 295
[16] Lucia Chiavola Birnbaum, *She is Everywhere,* (iUniverse, Lincoln, NE, 2005) 283
[17] Susanne Schaup, *Sophia, Aspects of the Divine Feminine,* (Niclolas-Hays, ME, 1997) 150
[18] Susanne Schaup, *Sophia, Aspects of the Divine Feminine,* (Niclolas-Hays, ME, 1997) 135
[19] Susanne Schaup, *Sophia, Aspects of the Divine Feminine,* (Niclolas-Hays, ME, 1997) xv
[20] *The Teachings of Buddha,* (Kenkyusha Printing, Tokyo, Japan, 1934) 30
[21] Frances Beer, *Julian of Norwich, Revelations-Motherhood of God,* D.S. Brewer, Cambridge, G.B., 1998) 61
[22] Tim Bulkeley, *Not Only A Father,* (Archer Press, Auckland, New Zealand, 2011) 118
[23] Tim Bulkeley, *Not Only A Father,* (Archer Press, Auckland, New Zealand, 2011) 119
[24] Tim Bulkeley, *Not Only A Father,* (Archer Press, Auckland, New Zealand, 2011) 121
[25] Lucia Chiavola Birnbaum, *She is Everywhere,* (iUniverse, Lincoln, NE, 2005) 201
[26] Tim Bulkeley, *Not Only A Father,* (Archer Press, Auckland, New Zealand, 2011) 120
[27] Tim Bulkeley, *Not Only A Father,* (Archer Press, Auckland, New Zealand, 2011) 115
[28] Tim Bulkeley, *Not Only A Father,* (Archer Press, Auckland, New Zealand, 2011) 116
[29] Tim Bulkeley, *Not Only A Father,* (Archer Press, Auckland, New Zealand, 2011) 9
[30] Sylvia Brown, *Father God, Co-Creator to Mother God,* (Hay House, CA, 2007) 95
[31] Tim Bulkeley, *Not Only A Father,* (Archer Press, Auckland, New Zealand, 2011) 98
[32] Craig S. Barnes, *In Search of the Lost Feminine,* (Fulcrum Publishing, Golden, CO, 206) 245
[33] Susanne Schaup, *Sophia, Aspects of the Divine Feminine,* (Niclolas-Hays, ME, 1997) 69
[34] Susanne Schaup, *Sophia, Aspects of the Divine Feminine,* (Niclolas-Hays, ME, 1997) 88

Sophia-Mother God

[35] Susan Cady, *Sophia, The Future of Feminist Spirituality,* (Harper & Row, New York, 1986) 77

[36] Susan Cady, *Sophia, The Future of Feminist Spirituality,* (Harper & Row, New York, 1986) 75

[37] Susan Cady, *Sophia, The Future of Feminist Spirituality,* (Harper & Row, New York, 1986) 60

[38] Susan Cady, *Sophia, The Future of Feminist Spirituality,* (Harper & Row, New York, 1986) 83

[39] Caitlin Matthews, *Sophia, Goddess of Wisdom, Bride of God*, (Quest Books, Wheaton, IL, 2001) 302

[40] Caitlin Matthews, *Sophia, Goddess of Wisdom, Bride of God*, (Quest Books, Wheaton, IL, 2001) 305

[41] Susan Cady, *Sophia, The Future of Feminist Spirituality,* (Harper & Row, New York, 1986) 85

[42] Caitlin Matthews, *Sophia, Goddess of Wisdom, Bride of God*, (Quest Books, Wheaton, IL, 2001) 47

[43] Susan Cady, *Sophia, The Future of Feminist Spirituality,* (Harper & Row, New York, 1986) 86

[44] Susan Cady, *Sophia, The Future of Feminist Spirituality,* (Harper & Row, New York, 1986) 81

[45] Susan Cady, *Sophia, The Future of Feminist Spirituality,* (Harper & Row, New York, 1986) 79

[46] Caitlin Matthews, *Sophia, Goddess of Wisdom, Bride of God*, (Quest Books, Wheaton, IL, 2001) 329

[47] Caitlin Matthews, *Sophia, Goddess of Wisdom, Bride of God*, (Quest Books, Wheaton, IL, 2001) 327

[48] Caitlin Matthews, *Sophia, Goddess of Wisdom, Bride of God*, (Quest Books, Wheaton, IL, 2001) 339

[49] Serenity Young, *An Anthology of Sacred Texts By and About Women*, (Crossroad Publishing, NY, 1993) 403

[50] Serenity Young, *An Anthology of Sacred Texts By and About Women*, (Crossroad Publishing, NY, 1993) 406

[51] Susan Cady, *Sophia, The Future of Feminist Spirituality,* (Harper & Row, New York, 1986) 83

[52] Serenity Young, *An Anthology of Sacred Texts By and About Women*, (Crossroad Publishing, NY, 1993) xv

[53] Susan Cady, *Sophia, The Future of Feminist Spirituality,* (Harper & Row, New York, 1986) 54

[54] Susan Cady, *Sophia, The Future of Feminist Spirituality,* (Harper & Row, New York, 1986) 25

[55] Susan Cady, *Sophia, The Future of Feminist Spirituality,* (Harper & Row, New York, 1986) 23

[56] Susan Cady, *Sophia, The Future of Feminist Spirituality,* (Harper & Row, New York, 1986) 33

[57] Manfred Hauke, *God or Goddess,*(Ignatius Press, S.F., CA, 1995) 254

[58] Susan Cady, *Sophia, The Future of Feminist Spirituality,* (Harper & Row, New York, 1986) 84

[59] Caitlin Matthews, *Sophia, Goddess of Wisdom, Bride of God,* (Quest Books, Wheaton, IL, 2001) 352

[60] Caitlin Matthews, *Sophia, Goddess of Wisdom, Bride of God,* (Quest Books, Wheaton, IL, 2001) 351

[61] Sylvia Brown, *Father God, Co-Creator to Mother God,* (Hay House, CA, 2007) 3

[62] Susan Cady, *Sophia, The Future of Feminist Spirituality,* (Harper & Row, New York, 1986) 17

Ma and Pa God - Mapah

[63] Elizabeth A. Johnson, *She Who Is,* (Crossroad Publishing, New York, 1986) 244

[64] Elizabeth A. Johnson, *She Who Is,* (Crossroad Publishing, New York, 1986) 134

[65] Susanne Schaup, *Sophia, Aspects of the Divine Feminine,* (Niclolas-Hays, ME, 1997) xx

[66] Elizabeth A. Johnson, *She Who Is,* (Crossroad Publishing, New York, 1986) 48

[67] Elizabeth A. Johnson, *She Who Is,* (Crossroad Publishing, New York, 1986) 183

[68] Lucia Chiavola Birnbaum, *She is Everywhere,* (iUniverse, Lincoln, NE, 2005) 119

[69] Lucia Chiavola Birnbaum, *She is Everywhere,* (iUniverse, Lincoln, NE, 2005) 253

[70] Elizabeth A. Johnson, *She Who Is,* (Crossroad Publishing, New York, 1986) 103

[71] Elizabeth A. Johnson, *She Who Is,* (Crossroad Publishing, New York, 1986) 180

[72] Elizabeth A. Johnson, *She Who Is,* (Crossroad Publishing, New York, 1986) 136

[73] Elizabeth A. Johnson, *She Who Is,* (Crossroad Publishing, New York, 1986) 36

[74] Elizabeth A. Johnson, *She Who Is,* (Crossroad Publishing, New York, 1986) 33

[75] Denye Robbins, *Reveolution, The Return of the Divine Feminine,*(Denye Robbins, CA, 2013) 17

[76] http://www.spiritwalkministry.com/earth_mother/goddess_movement

[77] Sonia Weiss, *The Complete Idiot's Guide to Women's History,*(BookEnds, IN, 2002) 8

[78] Manfred Hauke, *God or Goddess,*(Ignatius Press, S.F., CA, 1995) 20

[79] Manfred Hauke, *God or Goddess,*(Ignatius Press, S.F., CA, 1995) 151

[80] Manfred Hauke, *God or Goddess,*(Ignatius Press, S.F., CA, 1995) 164

[81] Manfred Hauke, *God or Goddess,*(Ignatius Press, S.F., CA, 1995) 47

[82] Manfred Hauke, *God or Goddess,*(Ignatius Press, S.F., CA, 1995) 105

[83] Manfred Hauke, *God or Goddess,*(Ignatius Press, S.F., CA, 1995) 247

[84] Manfred Hauke, *God or Goddess,*(Ignatius Press, S.F., CA, 1995) 107

[85] Elizabeth A. Johnson, *She Who Is*, (Crossroad Publishing, New York, 1986) 175

[86] Elizabeth A. Johnson, *She Who Is*, (Crossroad Publishing, New York, 1986) 179

[87] Patricia Taylor, *The Holy Spirit: The Feminine Nature of God*, (iUniverse, IN, 2009) 12

[88] Patricia Taylor, *The Holy Spirit: The Feminine Nature of God*, (iUniverse, IN, 2009) 13

Testimonies

[89] Margot Adler, *Drawing Down the Moon,* (Penguin Books, New York, 1986) 205

[90] Susanne Schaup, *Sophia, Aspects of the Divine Feminine,* (Niclolas-Hays, ME, 1997) 174

[91] Sun Myung Moon, *Cheon Seong Gyeong,* (Sunghwa Publishing Company, Korea, 2006) 68,69

[92] Sun Myung Moon, *World Scripture and the Teachings of Sun Myung Moon*, (UPF/Paragon, NY, 2007) 55

[93] Denye Robbins, Reveolution, *The Return of the Divine Feminine*, (Denye Robbins, CA, 2013) 18

Conclusion

[94] Elizabeth A. Johnson, *She Who Is*, (Crossroad Publishing, New York, 1986) 243

[95] Elizabeth A. Johnson, *She Who Is*, (Crossroad Publishing, New York, 1986) 258

[96] Elizabeth A. Johnson, *She Who Is*, (Crossroad Publishing, New York, 1986) 185

[97] Elizabeth A. Johnson, *She Who Is*, (Crossroad Publishing, New York, 1986) 185

[98] Neale Donald Walsch, *Conversations with God, Book 1*, (G.P. Putnam's Son, NY, 1996) 197

[99] Karen Speerstra, *Sophia, The Feminine Face of God,*(Michael Weise Productions, CA, 2011) 170

[100] J.J. Bachofen, *Myth, Religion and Mother Right*, (Princeton Univ. Press, NY, 1967) 139

CPSIA information can be obtained
at www.ICGtesting.com
Printed in the USA
FFOW03n1656250914
7601FF